Advance Praise
Millennials' Guide to Work

"There are certain things that $40k of student debt teaches you, like to never take out student loans for a degree. No matter the loan amount, however, there are things that you're never *actually* taught about work that you're somehow supposed to know. This guide answers a lot of those questions. Dr. Wisdom provides a guiding professional hand in an easily digested guide for even the shortest of attention spans (the Millennial plague) *without* the condescending tone that we Millennials are used to. Finally, someone believes in us! Save money on tuition – buy this book instead!"

Remy Watts, BS, MPA, BAMF, Actual Millennial (and yes, I'm for hire)

"*Millennials' Guide to Work* addresses the challenges and answers the questions you didn't know to ask, in an accessible, compassionate manner. Suddenly, navigating the work force seems far more manageable. Although this book is written for Millennials, in truth it contains useful guidance for workers of all ages. Dr. Wisdom's straightforward approach to naming and facing challenging situations provides a clear path to success, both interpersonally and within the workforce."

Kristina Hallett, PhD, ABPP, Clinical Psychologist, speaker, and author of *Own Best Friend: Eight Steps to a Life of Purpose, Passion, and Ease* and *BE AWESOME! Banish Burnout: Create Motivation from the Inside Out*

"The professional world would be a far more constructive, civilized, and efficient place if individuals entering it read *Millennials' Guide to Work*. Jennifer Wisdom imparts invaluable information in an entirely forthright and pragmatic manner with no preaching–just a focus on helping Millennials navigate often-challenging workplaces to help their true talents and valuable selves emerge."

Mary M. Mitchell, president, The Mitchell Organization

"Millennials' Guide to Work is relevant, useful and practical for all Millennials...it's a must read for success in the workplace and everyday situations."

David Mohammed, speaker, writer, and financial advisor

"It seems like every single day there's a new business book on how to 'deal with Millennials' but very rarely do you get information for Millennials on how to 'deal with everyone else.' Jennifer's book changes all of that. Covering a variety of topics that we should have learned in school but were never taught for some reason, *Millennials' Guide to Work* is a practical and action-oriented resource for anyone (millennial or otherwise) who wants to land a job, deal with coworkers, or just get better results in the workplace."

Andrew Tarvin, founder, Humor That Works

"I wish I had a guide like this when I started my career! I love how Dr. Wisdom provides actual phrases you can say in response to most every uncomfortable situation. This should be a required gift for every college intern and graduate so that they have it to help them with real-time questions or concerns on-the-job. "

Dawn Mahan, PMP, international speaker, author, non-profit board chair, founder & CEO of PMOtraining, LLC

"Dr. Wisdom has produced a thoughtful, practical, and easily accessible book for anyone looking to improve their performance in work settings. Its organization around specific and easy to understand problems with lists of extremely good suggestions for concrete approaches to address them will give readers many, many reasons to keep their copy close to their desks, for they will consult them frequently. Her experience, sensitivity to the complexities of the modern work place, and extensive knowledge of management and behavior science shine through on every page."

Richard R. Kilburg, PhD, clinical psychologist and author of *Executive Coaching, Executive Wisdom*, and *Virtuous Leaders*

"In this book, Dr. Wisdom provides a great many effective strategies for navigating the increasingly dynamic world of work, from identifying one's own values, interests and abilities, to engaging successfully with colleagues, bosses and organizations. As such, this is an invaluable resource for Millennials (or anyone else) looking for a job, for advancement, and/or for reliable ways to thrive in the workplace."

Philip J. Moore, PhD, Associate Professor of Applied Psychology, The George Washington University

"*Millennials' Guide to Work* contains all of the tips and tricks every Millennial wishes we learned in college, from building a professional network to setting honest goals. As a Millennial myself, I see how having this practical advice would have saved me from many awkward and confusing moments when I newly entered the workforce. This is a down-to-earth reference to keep accessible and handy for maneuvering through the workplace with grace, professionalism, and ease!"

Teresa Mona Miroslaw, Co-Founder, Elemental Healing

"The challenges one encounters in their professional lives rarely unfold like the orderly chapters of the latest business book. Dr. Wisdom presents viable solutions for a myriad of challenges, and has organized them in a way that allows the reader to navigate based on the situation at hand. It's like a Choose Your Own Adventure guide for professional problem solving!"

Rob Smith, Clinical Research Consultant

"In *Millennials' Guide to Work*, Jennifer Wisdom offers a refreshing roadmap to the most frequently asked questions a Millennial or anyone new to the work force would want to know in an easy to read and easy to digest format. Readers will benefit from the insights and tools Jennifer shares and be able to make immediate application as needed."

Eddie Turner, The Leadership Excelerator®, Best-Selling Author, and Podcast Host

"Dr. Wisdom's thoughtful, professional advice provides a range of options that will help both your short- and long-term goals. Her tone is encouraging and inclusive, and the enthusiasm with which she approaches these challenges provides a ray of hope. Most obstacles are not insurmountable, and Dr. Wisdom's options give you the opportunity to step back and figure out what solutions are right for you. I wish that I had a book like this when I started out, and I am so happy that this resource is available for others!"

Valerie Weaver, LCSW, Psychotherapist, Program Administrator, and Millennial

MILLENNIALS'
GUIDE TO
WORK

What No One Ever Told You About How to Achieve Success and Respect

WINDING PATHWAY BOOKS

JENNIFER P. WISDOM

Published by: Winding Pathway Books

WINDING PATHWAY BOOKS

ISBN (print): 978-1-7330977-0-3
ISBN (e-book): 978-1-7330977-1-0

Editing by: David Aretha
Book Design by: Deana Riddle at Bookstarter, Leila Creative, and Webnista
Photo Credit: Diego G. Diaz
For more information or bulk orders, visit: www.leadwithwisdom.com

Printed in the United States of America

Contents

PREFACE   1

FOREWORD   3

INTRODUCTION   7

HOW TO USE THIS BOOK   11

PART I. BASIC WORK SKILLS

CHALLENGE 1. UNDERSTANDING YOUR VALUES   15

CHALLENGE 2. BUILDING YOUR NETWORK   17

CHALLENGE 3. SETTING GOALS AND PRIORITIES   21

CHALLENGE 4. WHEN AND HOW TO OBTAIN A MENTOR   25

CHALLENGE 5. WHEN AND HOW TO OBTAIN A CAREER COACH   27

CHALLENGE 6. WHEN AND HOW TO OBTAIN A THERAPIST   31

CHALLENGE 7. HOW TO INTERVIEW FOR A JOB   35

CHALLENGE 8. STARTING A NEW JOB   39

CHALLENGE 9. UNDERSTANDING HIERARCHY
AT WORK AND WHEN TO GO AROUND IT   43

CHALLENGE 10. BUILDING RELATIONSHIPS WITH COLLEAGUES   47

CHALLENGE 11. SOCIAL MEDIA AT WORK   49

CHALLENGE 12. WORKING THROUGH DIFFERENCES   51

CHALLENGE 13. HOW TO HAVE DIFFICULT CONVERSATIONS   55

PART II. SELF-MANAGEMENT CHALLENGES

CHALLENGE 14. IT'S HARD TO FINISH TASKS   61

CHALLENGE 15. UNMOTIVATED AT WORK   63

CHALLENGE 16. FEEL ISOLATED   65

CHALLENGE 17. FEEL LIKE AN IMPOSTER   67

CHALLENGE 18. FEEL NEGATIVE ABOUT WORK   71

CHALLENGE 19. EASILY DISTRACTED   75

CHALLENGE 20. FEEL OVERWHELMED   77

CHALLENGE 21. WANT TO IMPROVE
TIME MANAGEMENT/ORGANIZATION   81

CHALLENGE 22. DIFFICULTY SAYING NO   83

CHALLENGE 23. BORED AT WORK   87

CHALLENGE 24. SHY/INTROVERTED   89

CHALLENGE 25. OVERLY CONCERNED OR
UNCONCERNED ABOUT OTHERS' FEELINGS   91

CHALLENGE 26. DIFFICULT TO ACCEPT PRAISE   93

CHALLENGE 27. HARD TO MAKE SMALL TALK   95

CHALLENGE 28. DIFFICULTY SPEAKING
IN PUBLIC/GIVING PRESENTATIONS   99

CHALLENGE 29. WANT FEEDBACK ON WORK PERFORMANCE   101

CHALLENGE 30. WANT MORE VISIBILITY   105

CHALLENGE 31. WANT TO INCREASE INFLUENCE   109

CHALLENGE 32. OFFICE ROMANCE FROM CRUSH TO BREAKUP   111

CHALLENGE 33. HOW MUCH PERSONAL
INFORMATION DO I SHARE WITH COLLEAGUES?   113

CHALLENGE 34. ASKING FOR A LETTER OF RECOMMENDATION   117

CHALLENGE 35. ASKING FOR A RAISE   121

CHALLENGE 36. YOU THINK IT'S TIME TO MOVE ON   125

CHALLENGE 37. ACCUSED OF WRONGDOING   129

PART III. COLLEAGUE CHALLENGES

CHALLENGE 38. YOU FEEL LIKE YOU ARE NOT HEARD   133

CHALLENGE 39. COLLEAGUES FREQUENTLY INTERRUPT YOU   135

CHALLENGE 40. MEETINGS ARE FRUSTRATING   139

CHALLENGE 41. ANNOYING OFFICE MATE   143

CHALLENGE 42. COLLEAGUE DOESN'T CONTRIBUTE   145

CHALLENGE 43. COLLEAGUES TAKE CREDIT FOR YOUR WORK   147

CHALLENGE 44. COLLEAGUES ARE EXTREMELY COMPETITIVE   149

CHALLENGE 45. BACKSTABBING   151

CHALLENGE 46. COLLEAGUES OVER-DISCLOSE
PERSONAL INFORMATION   153

CHALLENGE 47. GOSSIPY COLLEAGUES   157

CHALLENGE 48. COLLEAGUE PESTERS
YOU FOR A DATE OR HARASSES YOU   161

CHALLENGE 49. COLLEAGUES ARE AGGRESSIVE,
RACIST, SEXIST, HOMOPHOBIC, OR HOSTILE   165

PART IV. BOSS CHALLENGES

CHALLENGE 50. BOSS DOESN'T LEAD   169

CHALLENGE 51. BOSS TAKES CREDIT FOR YOUR WORK   173

CHALLENGE 52. BOSS GIVES
PREFERENTIAL TREATMENT TO OTHERS   175

CHALLENGE 53. BOSS DOES NOT MENTOR YOU   179

CHALLENGE 54. BOSS BULLIES YOU   183

CHALLENGE 55. BOSS ASKS ME TO DO
WORK OUTSIDE OF OFFICIAL DUTIES   185

CHALLENGE 56. BOSS INSULTS YOU IN FRONT OF OTHERS   187

CHALLENGE 57. BOSS LIES   191

CHALLENGE 58. BOSS HAS TEMPER TANTRUMS   193

CHALLENGE 59. BOSS HAS A SHORT ATTENTION SPAN   195

CHALLENGE 60. DON'T FEEL SUPPORTED BY BOSS   197

CHALLENGE 61. DON'T HAVE RESOURCES TO COMPLETE WORK   199

CHALLENGE 62. BOSS HAS UNREASONABLE EXPECTATIONS   201

CHALLENGE 63. BOSS UNDERMINES YOU   203

CHALLENGE 64. BOSS SUGGESTS IT'S TIME TO MOVE ON   207

CHALLENGE 65. NEW BOSS   209

CHALLENGE 66. NOT SURE WHERE TO GO FOR
HELP WITH A PROBLEM   211

FOR FURTHER READING   213

ACKNOWLEDGEMENTS   219

Preface

Everyone wants a job where they can shine, be recognized for who they are, work with wonderful colleagues, contribute great things, and, of course, get rewarded with pay and the ability to grow. It's fantastic when you find that kind of work. In my experience, a job like that makes my heart sing!

For many of us, however, our jobs do not make our hearts sing. We may feel overworked, underpaid, disrespected, or frustrated. Further, there are many things about work that *no one ever tells you*. No one told me how to build a network – and why a network is so important. No one told me what to do when I wasn't getting feedback on my work. Definitely no one told me what to do when my boss had a temper tantrum! Or that the responsibility for my career lies squarely on me. As I made my way through the work world and up the career ladder, I encountered many colleagues, staff, and students who had similar challenges. Like me, they also struggled with how to be proactive at work, and how to respond to situations we never imagined we'd encounter.

No job is perfect, but my experience has taught me that nearly every job can be improved. We can always improve our own skills in communication, negotiation, teamwork, and effectiveness. The end goal is never a job where there is zero tension and where everything works perfectly: every job is a work in progress because the nature of the work changes, technology improves, staff leave, new staff begin, and we ourselves learn and grow. I've learned to deal with the stickiest of situations both from my plentiful mistakes and my confident successes. As I became more senior and started mentoring others, I had the honor of being a sounding board for them as they encountered similar situations.

One of the critical issues I see across generations is the issue of respect: I hear frequently from Millennials, Gen Xers and Baby Boomers that everyone feels disrespected by the other generations. I believe everyone deserves respect. Ultimately, respect is about *regard,*

1

about saying "I see you" to others, and knowing deeply that everyone has something to offer, and everyone has something to learn. This book is designed to help you give and earn that respect at work.

I am writing this book for you. I want to share with you all the things no one ever tells you about work, including how to approach and remedy many of the challenges you might encounter. Regardless of what kind of work you do – finance, construction, marketing, administration, or any of the million other jobs out there – I want you to know that whatever comes your way at work, you are not alone and you are NEVER powerless.

Jennifer Wisdom
April 2019

Foreword

A few months back, I was contacted by a Millennial reporter from *Lifehacker* asking me to discuss healthy self-care for Millennials working from home. What later resulted was a hilarious article entitled "*How to Work From Home Without Falling Into a Pit of Despair,*" in which my reporter confessed to shutting herself up in her New York apartment wearing the same yoga pants for days on end, not speaking to any other human beings lest she force herself into weekly Pilates classes so as to not become a complete shut-in. I laughed knowingly; as a fellow Millennial who is extremely grateful to be self-employed, I knew very well how isolating independent work could be. And given how much the work landscape has changed, allowing tech entrepreneurs, writers, and others to work from home, the piece was timely indeed.

Then a few months later, this same reporter reached out again. This time she was asking about dealing with toxic colleagues. I realized that while as a psychologist I certainly understood time-tested strategies for effective communication, dispute management, and social intelligence to deal with these scenarios, I had effectively removed such scenarios from my life altogether. I worked from home, disconnected my office phone number, set up an email auto-responder that said due to my hectic schedule I'd get back to them later if it was important and possibly not at all in the event of media interviews and random inquiries. Talk about going off the work grid—or trying to!

The reality is that in this age of digital connectedness and often emotional disconnectedness, we are all trying to carve out time to live our best most fulfilled lives. What is incredible about the Millennial generation is that we don't settle for second best and want vocations and not just jobs. We care about social impact and missions, but in so doing are ever distracted by the essentials. Rent is sky high, savings are low, and competition is intense. We are trying to make ends meet without losing our souls in the process. But inevitably there are bosses to please, toxic colleagues to avoid, and endless emails to sift through.

We are managing our own expectations and keeping up with a Kardashian world of social media. Meanwhile, our old college roommate is moving into a gorgeous new home while we are still crashing with our parents.

A roadmap for navigating the choppy waters of work is much needed, and indeed it is what Dr. Jennifer Wisdom provides readers with in this fantastic and highly digestible guide! I had the honor of working with Dr. Wisdom what feels like forever ago as a young college student. I acutely remember the anxiety of wanting to do my best, getting the best letters of recommendation I could, and going on to the graduate school of my dreams. Working with college students and Millennials now as a therapist, I laugh as I remember the anguish that sometimes came with "messing up," especially in front of our professional role models.

Just the other week I was talking to an anxious therapy client who was worried she'd messed up in front of a future mentor. I retold the story of my own complete panic working as a research assistant for none other than Dr. Wisdom herself! I remember at the time gladly stepping up to the plate to complete all sorts of odds and ends for our research team from photocopying hundred page grant applications to updating references and research articles in computer systems. The project that stumped me: Dr. Wisdom had brought in a tray of beautiful chocolate cupcakes for a departmental gathering with a separate container of frosting. My task: frost the cupcakes. I kid you not, I had never done this before!! I literally grew up in a household where cupcakes had never been baked. What was I going to do?!

To be honest, I don't even remember how the situation was resolved. Likely, I botched a few cupcakes and Dr. Wisdom took over from there with grace and kindness. At the time, I was horrified. And yet, as I write this, I am laughing out loud at what a big deal it seemed like at the time. The truth is there are countless unexpected moments in our professional lives and many of the things that seemed insurmountable at one point in time are truly drops in the bucket now. It is about equipping ourselves with the best tools possible and reminding ourselves to practice self-compassion and have a healthy dose of humor and humility throughout it all.

4

I can't tell you how excited I am that such a resource finally exists! As a Millennial therapist and writer, I know what a gap there is in addressing work challenges for this unique population. And while many books will have you sifting through pages of irrelevant material, Dr. Wisdom boils it down to the nuts and bolts of getting out of sticky situations. I'm positive without a shadow of doubt that I could have used this reference well over a decade ago when all I wanted to do was quickly Google "cupcake frosting for beginners!"

Goali Saedi Bocci, Ph.D., writes the popular Millennial Media blog for *Psychology Today* and is the author of *PhDiva, The Social Media Workbook for Teens, The Digital Detox Deck*, and the upcoming title, *The Millennial Mental Health Toolbox*. Learn more at www.drgoali.com.

Introduction

Millennials were born between approximately 1980 and 1996. You followed Generation X (born 1965–1980), who followed the Baby Boomers (born 1946–1964), who followed the Silent Generation (born 1922–1945). You have probably heard of traits typically attributed to Millennials, such as confidence, tolerance, and social consciousness on the positive side, and entitlement and self-centeredness on the negative side. Millennials are also the first "digital native" generation, which creates challenges when working with those of us who have different experiences of technology. In my personal experience, I have found Millennials to be optimistic and adventurous, while somewhat skeptical and unsure of how to best move forward.

Something all generations have in common is that there are numerous challenges to being successful and earning respect at work. Many of us – not just Millennials – have experienced the challenge of needing experience to get a job but also needing a job to get experience. Many of us have struggled with how to manage our own thoughts, beliefs, and actions, as sometimes we can be our own worst enemy. We may have encountered challenging colleagues, challenging bosses or both. Maybe we feel like we aren't taken seriously because we are young. Or we don't know how to advance in our field when it seems like we aren't getting opportunities to shine. Other obstacles are unique to Millennials, including the challenge of having enormous opportunities of technology and media and a faster pace of work when our bosses may not fully understand or appreciate these opportunities.

Further, Millennials are not a homogenous group. Some Millennials are sophomores in college as I write this, while others are in their 30s and may have 15 or more years of professional work experience. Some are transitioning from college mentality to work mentality; others are transitioning from being a worker to becoming a manager. Still, a satisfying work life doesn't happen automatically. You have to look for it – and, often make it happen yourself. It's almost never a smooth path, so it's important to recognize and try to avoid large obstacles. At the same time, everyday issues are an amazing source for learning about who we are, our values, and how we can strive to better ourselves.

Despite the multitude of books on management and leadership, there are remarkably few books on how to get through the day-to-day challenges that we all face – and often spell the difference between being happy and successful at work or just dragging yourself through the day. For example, you get your dream job – and find your boss doesn't mentor you as you had hoped. In fact, your boss hardly has time for you at all! Or you really want to get somewhere – but where? If you're not sure how to set goals and take steps to reach them, you can get really stuck. Or you have that coworker everyone dreads. They keep taking credit for your work while barely doing anything themselves. That stinks!

That's where this book comes in.

I have assembled more than 60 day-to-day work challenges Millennials are likely to encounter and action steps for how to address them. Some challenges are seemingly minor, such as you feel isolated or you want more visibility in the office. Other challenges are more severe, such as experiencing sexual harassment or being accused of wrongdoing. Some challenges you may have to manage within yourself, such as changing your attitude or habits. Others are about working with your colleagues, and still others are about how to deal with a challenging boss. If your work involves dealing with other people, at some point you will encounter at least some of these challenges.

For each of these challenges, there are 10 to 20 action steps you can take. You don't have to take them all at once; review the "How to use this book" section for suggestions about how to work with the action steps.

Part I of *Millennials' Guide to Work* includes what I call basic work skills, including understanding your values around work, tips on interviewing for and starting a new job, and how to set priorities and goals. Since we all need help sometimes, it also includes a section on when and how to get help from a mentor, a coach, and a therapist, and choosing when each one is appropriate. These skills will set you up for success regardless of what field of work you are in, and whatever your current level of seniority.

Part II describes self-management challenges. These are the challenges where we may not know something about ourselves, or we may be getting in our own way. These challenges include action steps to take when we are bored at work, feel isolated, have difficulty speaking in public, or feel like an imposter.

Next is Part III, colleague challenges. When the philosopher Sartre said "Hell is other people," he might have been referring to the coworker who always stinks up the break room with fish or burned popcorn. It feels challenging, though, when we have an annoying office mate, competitive colleagues, or gossipy teammates who don't do their work. Approaching these challenges in a positive and diplomatic way can work wonders at improving your work environment.

Finally, in Part IV, we discuss challenges with the boss. In this section, "boss" refers to your supervisor, someone you report to, or someone who is in charge. Although some challenges with bosses are similar to those of coworkers, the differential power dynamic makes boss problems even more challenging to address, especially if you're very junior. I have had wonderful and inspiring bosses, but this section describes what to do if your boss insults you, doesn't mentor you, or is otherwise challenging.

When I was early in my career, work challenges led me to the library or bookstore. I read books on how to deal with difficult work situations and walked into work the next day ready to address any problem that came my way. I've included a reading list of my favorites as well as newer books that provide novel perspectives on work challenges. These are in the "For further reading" section.

How did I come up with these challenges? I have personally experienced some of them in 30+ years of adult work. I have also coached many Millennials on many of these challenges as they described them to me. Some have been described to me by coworkers, students, friends, and clients and we brainstormed potential solutions together. In each of these situations, I have had a front-row seat to see how all of us address these challenges in ways ranging from extremely effective (high-five!) to oh-my-god-how-could-I-have-done-that. I'm giving you only the good options! The goal is addressing challenges effectively, with integrity, personal growth, and hopefully a little grace.

My hope is that your work life will be always filled with joy, accomplishment, recognition for your achievements, and supportive colleagues and bosses. For the times when you're facing challenges, however, this book is here for you.

How to use this book

This is not a book best read cover to cover. I encourage you to review the table of contents and identify a challenge you are currently having or recently experienced. Turn to those pages to start finding a solution!

Each challenge includes a brief description and at least 10 possible solutions that you may want to try. Many times, you can see success after trying just one option. You'll see some solutions repeated across different challenges because they're likely to be helpful for many problems. For complex challenges, you may want to attempt several interventions at the same time. I suggest using a little bit of the scientific method as you try this process: After you identify the challenge you're having, visualize what it would look like for you once the issue is resolved. Then as you try out solutions, you have an ideal to measure progress against. It's helpful if you take an approach of curiosity; pretend you're Sherlock Holmes (the cool Benedict Cumberbatch version!) trying to figure out and solve the problem.

It's important to have patience and give the solutions a little bit of time to work. Some ideas that you try won't solve the problem but will make it a little better – that's still success! If you don't feel comfortable trying a solution or if it works partially or not at all, try something else. Some of the solutions are very low risk, such as changing your expectations of the other person. Others can appear more challenging, such as directly discussing a concern with a colleague or asking for a raise from your boss. Start with solutions that feel lower risk to you, and work your way up to more challenging solutions.

As you work through possible solutions, you'll get better at reading situations, responding to people you work with, building networks, and applying solutions effectively. There will sometimes be political situations in which there is a game being played around you that you don't fully get. Observe, be patient, clarify your own boundaries, and learn. The more you know what you want, the more you'll be able to achieve your goals. If you're not sure what you want, that's okay too –

that's a perfect place to be while you're in your 20s and 30s. The goal of the strategies in this book is to help you develop skills that will serve you well as you continue to move forward at work.

It's important to remember a few basic rules of work that will never steer you wrong:

1. Never say anything bad about anyone at work to anyone at work. (Do your venting at home or with friends.)

2. Write emails as if they will be printed in the newspaper or used in a court case (because they might be).

3. Be honest *and* diplomatic with everyone, including yourself.

4. Be patient. Sometimes people are working on your behalf to make things better and you don't even know it.

5. Be curious about yourself and seek constant self-improvement.

6. Remember that we all have struggles. Be kind and respectful.

Each of you reading this book is a unique person with talents to share with the world. My hope is that this book can make it easier for you to do so. Good luck improving your work life!

Part I. Basic Work Skills

Challenge 1.
Understanding your values

Some of us value a competitive environment that keeps us motivated, whereas others want a collegial and friendly environment. Some people don't mind specified work times, and others bristle at anything that feels like micromanagement. Often we don't even consider our values until they are being challenged in some way. Values are statements of what we find important, valuable, or useful. Taking some time to clarify what we authentically value and where we draw the line can be important to guide us as we move forward in our careers.

1. Often employers are looking for values such as dependability, positive attitude, professionalism, loyalty, motivation, honesty, and adaptability. Starting with those values, how do you feel you measure up? How much are those values important to you?

2. Ask friends and family members who know you well what they value and identify anything that feels true for you.

3. Review values statements for your organization and for other similar organizations to identify what feels right for you and what doesn't feel right for you.

4. Consider difficult situations in your past when you've had to make a decision. What principles guided your decision? What beliefs did you rely upon? If you can't recall a difficult situation or identify principles and beliefs you considered, it may point to a need to be more present or to begin documenting your experiences.

5. Ask a trusted colleague about their values and how they apply their values in day-to-day work.

6. Consider whether your spiritual, religious, or cultural beliefs/experiences may impact your values.

7. Consider what brought up your concern about values: Is someone pressuring you to do something that goes against your values? Are you uncomfortable with an aspect of a work requirement or your work environment? Do you feel like you just need to have clarity? Understanding *why* you want to clarify your values might give you some direction.

8. A conversation about values is also a good time to consider your future: Do you see yourself continuing in your field as a worker or as a manager? It's okay if you're not sure now. If you know you prefer one or the other, though, it's helpful to keep that in mind as you move forward because you will have decision points along the way where you need to choose a direction.

9. When you are faced with a situation at work that is challenging, try to identify what is most important for you: to do the right thing, to be fair, to help others, to be right, to avoid trouble? How might these preferences reflect your values?

10. Know that your values will likely become more clear over time, and trust that you are on the right path.

See also: Challenge 3: Setting goals and priorities
Challenge 22: Difficulty saying no

Take Action: What are your values? From your values, where did you pick them up? Take notice of values that come from society, family, religion and decide if you will keep them as your own or create new ones.

Challenge 2.
Building your network

You may often hear that it's important to build your network, but you may not know how to do that or why. A network of colleagues can be a source of support, strategies, job opportunities, helpful information, problem solving, collaborations, and feedback that will help you work effectively and advance in the field if you wish. People in your networks help you – and you help them. Good networks include people inside and outside of your organization, people in your field and outside of it, and people at different levels of seniority. Plan to be open and friendly to lots of people to build a strong network.

1. Approach building a network as a way to make lifelong relationships with people who share your interests and goals and with people who think and work differently than you.

2. Talk to someone you trust outside of work, even outside your field, for an external opinion on how to build networks. Ask them what social media they use (such as LinkedIn) for building networks and start building your own online network.

3. Map your current network, including who you network with who is junior to you, colleagues with you, and senior to you. Identify where you would like more individuals and find them. Include people both within and outside your organization. Your professional network is likely much larger than your organization's network. Work on filling gaps by meeting people to strengthen your network.

4. Invite a colleague to work with you on a project to get to know them better.

5. Offer something you may have to a colleague who is in need. For example, if a colleague is interested in learning more about a topic and you know someone who works in that area, offer to introduce them. Mutual sharing – of information, tips, opportunities, and support – strengthens networks faster than anything else!

6. Identify people in your field who are doing interesting work and invite them to coffee or a 15-minute phone conversation about their career path.

7. Consider taking a professional development or certification class at work or in the community to meet people in your line of work. Keep in mind it's important to meet people at your level of seniority, people junior to you, and people more senior to you.

8. Commit to a goal of saying hello to one new person every day. After you feel more comfortable saying hello, commit to starting a conversation, and then to asking someone to have coffee.

9. Ask friendly colleagues if they'd be open to a networking lunch periodically where you have a book club, review a recent article about your field, or discuss recent challenges.

10. Set up meetings to get a chance to talk with people and ask them questions. Sometimes it's easier when we can approach talking to someone as a work requirement instead of as our own initiative.

11. Identify the top publications in your field and read them. Reach out to authors or people quoted in those publications to ask professional questions and potentially develop a relationship.

12. Use social media that is typical for your field, such as LinkedIn or Instagram. Always be professional. Consider creating a separate account for professional purposes.

13. Identify other people at work who seem to have good networks and build relationships with them. Ask them for tips on building networks. Be sure to be genuine.

14. Attend conferences in your field, and make a point to introduce yourself to at least five people you don't know. You have to put yourself out there to build networks. Prepare before networking events with a few questions or conversation starters. For example, start conversations by saying, "Tell me about what you do at your company."

See also: Challenge 10: Building relationships with colleagues
Challenge 12: Working through differences
Challenge 24: Shy/introverted
Challenge 27: Hard to make small talk

Take Action: Go ahead and research events that allow you to network with people you want to get to know better. What are 3-5 events you can attend in the next 6 months?

Challenge 3.
Setting goals and priorities

As a longtime nerd, every December I review the past year and set goals for the new year. I set goals in areas of Work, Writing, Fitness, Financial, and Fun/Travel. I don't always achieve everything, but as I review my goals several times throughout the year, I get more done than I would without a list. It also helps me say no to activities that are not my priorities.

1. Consider setting SMART goals: Goals that are **S**pecific (you know exactly what you want changed), **M**easurable (you'll know when you have completed it), **A**chievable (it's something you can complete), **R**elevant (it's a goal that is important to you), and **T**ime-bound (your target date for completing each step and the whole goal). Write them down.

2. Set goals that have a variety of challenge: some may be easy to reach, and others can be stretch goals (stretch goals require you to go beyond your comfort zone to work harder). Too many easy goals and you won't be challenged enough; too many stretch goals and you may get too discouraged.

3. Set short-term and long-term goals: some that can be achieved within weeks; others within a month or two; and big goals to achieve within a year or two. Consider breaking big goals down into smaller chunks with shorter target dates for completion.

4. Consider what your organization may need that you could incorporate into your professional goals. Ensure you collaborate with key people when your goals affect others.

5. Set goals related to work as well as goals related to other areas such as networking, fitness, diet, community involvement, social causes, or travel. You may also be able to double-dip; for example, goals to increase your professional network and exercise can both be addressed by joining your organization's running group. Take action!

6. Ask people you admire and who are successful about how they set goals and how they achieve their goals.

7. Consider your Big Life Purpose – why you believe you are on this planet – and then set big goals from there. Don't worry if the goals are too big; you'll grow into them! If you don't have a Big Life Purpose, that's okay as well. Keep moving toward things you want and feel drawn to that will help you grow and become a better person, and your Big Life Purpose will work itself out.

8. Consider what you may need to complete your goals, such as professional development, additional training, consultation, or something else. Ask around to find someone who can advise.

9. Sometimes goals may need to change, and that is okay. Make sure you change goals for good reasons, not just because you're discouraged.

10. Once you put your goals together, identify your plans to reach them. You may want to break them down into smaller steps. Put target dates for steps and goals in your calendar or appointment book so you will remember. The more you integrate achieving goals into your everyday life, the more you will achieve.

11. Periodically reassess your goals, such as on your birthday, end of year, or some other time. See how much you've achieved, reflect on what is in progress, note what has been challenging, and let go of what's no longer important to you.

See also: Challenge 4: When and how to obtain a mentor
Challenge 15: Unmotivated at work
Challenge 20: Feel overwhelmed
Challenge 23: Bored at work

Take Action: How will you take action towards your goals today, this week and this month?

Challenge 4.
When and how to obtain a mentor

Sometimes we all need help. The next few challenges identify the differences between a mentor, a coach, and a therapist, including when you might need each of these, how to find one, and how to work with them. A mentor is someone who is committed to your growth and professional development. Typically, mentors help you learn what you need to know on the job and how to improve. A mentor is different from a coach in that a coach typically is paid and has very structured meetings focused on a specific goal. It's also different from therapy in that a therapist typically addresses past harms and current coping strategies as opposed to career advancement.

1. A good first step to finding a mentor is to figure out what you would like help with: general professional advice, sticky situations, technical skills, advancement, or something else. Then you can start looking for someone who is especially knowledgeable about that area.

2. See if your organization has a mentoring program, new employee orientation, or early career networking meetings. Those are excellent places to find mentors.

3. Ideally, your mentor has your best interests and professional development in mind, but they are human too and may be interested in learning information from you or steer you in certain directions. If you feel your mentor is not acting in your best interests, you may want to step back and reassess.

4. Respect your mentor's time. Be on time and prepared for meetings. Do your homework first (don't ask them to tell you things a simple Internet search could uncover). You may want to bring a written list of what you want to discuss.

5. Follow up on their advice. There are few things a mentor loves to hear more than "Your advice was so helpful. It really made a difference."

6. Be aware that it's rare to find a single mentor who can meet all of your needs. You may find one person who can help you with general professional advice, and another one who can advise on sticky situations. Go slowly on questions, and ask your mentor how they would like to proceed.

7. Some mentorships last a lifetime, others for a short time. If you need to end a mentoring relationship for whatever reason, it's always polite to thank the person for being there for you and let them know how much they have helped you.

8. Help your mentor out when you can. Send them news items or articles you came across that they might be interested in, or pass along non-confidential information they might find helpful to their goals. Ask them directly how you can help them.

9. If you find a mentor isn't particularly helpful, be specific and ask for what you are looking for. Mentors want to be helpful and will likely let you know if they can't help on a specific topic.

10. Pass it on. Regardless of your position and seniority, you know something someone doesn't. Be kind and mentor others. It will help you build positive, collegial relationships, and it will make the world a little friendlier for all of us.

See also: Challenge 5: When and how to obtain a career coach
Challenge 6: When and how to obtain a therapist
Challenge 13: How to have difficult conversations
Challenge 53: Boss does not mentor you

Take Action: Who mentors you? What's one step you can take right now to get the mentoring you would like?

Challenge 5.
When and how to obtain a career coach

Coaches are experts, usually paid, who help you tackle certain problems. Coaches are less likely to have any conflict of interest, as their primary goal is helping you achieve what you want to achieve. They are typically action-oriented, and want to help you achieve change. This is different from a mentor, who often is a volunteer and who offers less structured support. A coach is also different from a therapist, whose primary focus is on coping and healing.

1. You can find coaches through the American Psychological Association (apa.org), the International Coaching Federation (icf.org), your state psychological association, and by searching online. Note there is no standard certification for coaches.

2. You may want a coach who is certified as a coach or licensed as a psychologist, someone who is a professional in your field (e.g., finance, medicine), or all of the above. Look for a coach who has experience working with people at your level of seniority and with the kinds of problems you would like assistance with. If you're not sure, just ask.

3. When you contact a prospective coach, ask about their style and strategies. Some coaches have a warm, supportive style, whereas others have a more direct and confrontative style. If you have a preference, let them know and ask if they can accommodate.

4. Ask about the prospective coach's strategies. Do they have a formal assessment or interview before you begin? Do they tend to have a similar structure for each session? How do they consider homework? How do they balance inquiry and advice-giving?

5. If cost is important, ask about how the coach charges for services. Many coaches offer a "bundle," such as a single price for five or 10 sessions. Be sure to ask about what happens if you do not complete all sessions; you may be able to take a break but often will not be entitled to a refund. Consider whether your workplace may support the cost of a coach.

6. Be clear on what you want from a coach if at all possible. Usually coaches will help with dilemmas (such as whether to apply for a new job or not) or puzzles (such as how to build a better relationship with your boss or how to better balance work and life). If you're not sure what you want, then let the prospective coach know that and ask for assistance.

7. Coaches ask a lot of questions, and they help you uncover answers in yourself. Most coaches assume you are resourceful and talented in managing your own life. Don't be put off if the coach asks lots (and lots!) of questions, but if you prefer a more directive style, let them know.

8. A coach should never discount the significance or importance of your challenge. If you feel dismissed or talked down to, end the relationship and find someone who completely supports you.

9. Many coaches assign homework. Work with them on what you are comfortable with. Often the homework is for you to think through challenging issues, or to practice strategies discussed in coaching sessions. You'll get more out of coaching if you do the homework.

10. Coaches will provide you with feedback regarding how you present within the session; for example, if you are snippy, late, or reject feedback, you will likely receive that feedback. If it is hard for you to receive feedback, let the coach know and ask to work on that.

11. Be curious about yourself and be open to learning. Coaching can be an effective way to help you reduce frustration and improve your skills!

See also: Challenge 3: Setting goals and priorities
                  Challenge 4: When and how to obtain a mentor
                  Challenge 6: When and how to obtain a therapist
                  Challenge 53: Boss does not mentor you

Take action: Do you know anyone who has worked with a coach? Ask around to see what their experiences are before you decide this is right for you.

Challenge 6.
When and how to obtain a therapist

If your needs go beyond what a coach or mentor can reasonably manage; if you're often distressed to the point of tears, sleep problems, eating problems, or severe anxiety; or if you find that you're encountering the same patterns of dysfunction at work repeatedly, therapy might be a good choice. A therapist helps you understand how past experiences can be affecting your current functioning, and helps you uncover patterns and figure out how to cope with them. Therapy often includes more personal conversation than you would be likely to get into with a mentor or a coach, and is focused on your whole life, not just work.

1. Therapists can be psychologists, social workers, psychiatrists, or counselors. These groups have a lot of overlap and some differences in focus. For example, psychiatrists can prescribe medicine, psychologists (PhD and PsyD) are more likely to be able to conduct psychological testing, and social workers often (but not always) focus on family and relationships.

2. You can find a therapist by asking friends, your physician, a university psychiatry/psychology/counseling department, or a large clinic for a referral.

3. You could also contact your health insurance plan if you have one or online networks such as the American Psychological Association, your state psychological association, National Association of Social Workers, or the American Psychiatric Association, but it is best to use those lists as a starting point, not an end point.

4. Therapy requires trust. Look for a therapist who has expertise and experience in treating the kinds of issues you are presenting, whether trauma, anxiety, depression, or something

else. Ask about how much they have treated people like you, whether that means age, race/ethnicity, gender, sexual orientation, religion, or other characteristics if that is a concern for you.

5. Many people want a therapist who is similar to them in gender, race, or sexual orientation, especially if they have concerns related to any of those identities. It's definitely possible to make significant progress with someone who is different from you; it's most important to have a trusting and professional relationship.

6. You may want to ask the therapist how long they anticipate you will be in therapy to address your issues. Note therapy typically takes longer than coaching or mentoring, depending on the kinds of situations you would like assistance with. The therapist may only be able to answer that question after a few sessions when they more fully understand your needs.

7. Ask about cost. Sometimes costs can be offset by your health insurance.

8. A therapist should never discount the significance or importance of your challenge. If you feel dismissed or talked down to, end the relationship and find someone who completely supports you.

9. A therapist who is not a physician may recommend you consult with a physician for medication. If you have any concerns about medication, talk to the therapist first. Medication can be enormously helpful for some people.

10. It's important to be open with your therapist about how you are or are not making progress, how you feel about whether therapy is helpful, and if you want to end the therapeutic relationship. Therapists do not take it personally if you want to discuss ending therapy. They are there to support your personal growth!

See also: Challenge 4: When and how to obtain a mentor
            Challenge 5: When and how to obtain a career coach
            Challenge 13: How to have difficult conversations

Take Action: Do you know anyone who has worked with a therapist? Ask around outside of work to see what their experiences are before you decide this is right for you.

Challenge 7.
How to interview for a job

Once you are being considered for a job, you'll likely need to have an online or in-person interview. Although many people stress about the interview because you are being judged for your fit for the job, an interview is also your opportunity to check out the company and to see if you are interested in working for them. Preparation and practice will go a long way toward being seen as a top candidate!

1. Prepare for your interview by reviewing the company, its products or services, its leadership team, and the team you're applying to work with if possible. If you know anyone who works at the company, ask questions about what it's like to work there.

2. If you can get information in advance on who you will meet, check out their social media or their profile on the company webpage so you will have information about their role in the company and any background information that may be useful (such as you went to the same college).

3. Show up early! It's a great idea to plan to arrive an hour early and do any final preparation at a coffee shop around the corner if that's possible. This also gives you some cushion in case anything goes wrong on your commute.

4. Hopefully this goes without saying, but only you should go to your job interview. An executive I know told me about an interview candidate she was considering hiring, only to find that the candidate's parents were waiting outside. Prepare together and celebrate together, but go to the interview by yourself.

5. Prepare for questions you will likely be asked and practice how you will answer them. Common interview questions include:

a) Tell me about your experience/education/thesis. b) Why do you want to work here? c) Where do you see yourself in five years? d) What questions do you have for me?

6. Have questions to ask the interviewer. These can include: a) Can you give me some examples of the most and least desirable aspects of [the company's] culture? b) How do you define and measure success for this position? c) (at end of interview) Now that we've discussed my qualifications, what concerns do you have about my fit for the position? (d) (at end of interview) What are the next steps in the hiring process?/When can I expect to hear back?/What is the anticipated hiring date?

7. In the interview, focus on the work. Interviews are generally not a good time to ask about salary, vacation time, or other benefits unless the interviewer brings them up.

8. If the interviewer wants to move forward with an offer, they may ask you about your start date or salary expectations. It would be good to have a general idea of what you are looking for, but you don't have to negotiate on the spot. A good response can be, "When do you need an answer?"

9. Make sure you are all set for an interview as if it were your first day of school: plan what you'll wear, transportation, what you'll eat, extra pens and paper, water to drink, and any special concerns like medication you might need. Make sure you can easily carry your bag and that you have comfortable shoes in case you're taken on a walking tour.

10. Always be nice to everyone you meet on an interview. You won't always know who they are at the time. In addition, many workplaces want to know the opinions of everyone who interacted with you, including administrative staff.

11. When you complete the interview, write thank you letters to everyone you meet. I prefer handwritten as they make a bigger

impact, but you could email them. Make sure you don't write everyone the exact same letter; find a way to personalize each one.

12. Practice interviewing with someone you trust who has been employed in a similar kind of job. Ask them to comment on your handshake, your eye contact, your tone (speak up!), and the content of your answers.

13. Even if you ace the interview, you may not get the job and you may not hear any feedback. That doesn't mean you did anything wrong. You can follow up with an email or phone call to request the status of your application for the position, but don't take it personally if you don't hear back.

See also: Challenge 13: How to have difficult conversations
            Challenge 27: Hard to make small talk
            Challenge 34: Asking for a letter of recommendation

Take Action: Think back to your last job interview. What would you have done differently knowing what you know now? How can you use that information to improve the next time around?

Challenge 8.
Starting a new job

It's so exciting – you're starting a new job! Whether this is your first-ever job or you're used to this, a new job is still an exciting opportunity to get started on the right foot. Being prepared can also help reduce anxiety of a first day.

1. Make a list of why you wanted the job and what your goals are. File it away to look at in three months. Update it and review it in six and 12 months as well. Set reminders in your calendar so you remember.

2. Before your first day, create a list of your questions for the first week, including about direct deposit, expected work hours, and where the cafeteria is. Be prepared to add to that list as the week continues.

3. Make sure you are all set for the first day of a new job as if it were your first day of school: plan what you'll wear, look at transportation schedules, plan for meals, and bring a water bottle and any special items you might need. Dress comfortably and in a similar style to the people who interviewed you.

4. If you need any accommodations for a disability, talk early to the appropriate office so you have a point of contact and details on how to ask for help if you need it. This sets you up for success.

5. Consider using humor, such as by referring to yourself as "the newbie" and letting people know you're new when you ask questions. First impressions are important!

6. Read the excellent book *The First 90 Days: Proven Strategies for Getting Up to Speed Faster and Smarter*, by Michael D. Watkins, which walks you through how to approach a first job (details listed in the "For further reading" section).

7. Introduce yourself kindly and generously to everyone you meet. Let people know your name, job title, and your manager or the team you're working on. At this point, you don't know who they are and you never know where they will be in the future.

8. Be prepared to answer questions about where you were before you started this job. If you took time off or had a difficult experience before starting this job, practice what you will say so that you can say it breezily and without emotions until you get to know people better.

9. Early on in the process, identify your chain of command (who you report to and whom your boss reports to, etc.), the organization's policy manual, and channels your organization has for whistle blowing, reporting abuse, reporting harassment, and bullying. You can ask about these casually so it doesn't appear you are anticipating trouble. You might want to say, "Could you point me to the organization's policies? I'd like to take a look so I can let you know any questions." Knowing the rules is enormously helpful, especially if challenges come up.

10. Remember the individuals who interviewed you, and when you see them at work the first time, say something kind.

11. Talk to someone you trust outside of work for an outside opinion and a pep talk for your new journey. Make sure it's someone who has experience in professional environments and who has your best interests in mind.

12. You may want to consider obtaining a coach who can help you through starting a new job.

13. Reward yourself with something pleasant after you finish your first day, whether dinner with your partner or friends, a special dessert, or something else. You deserve it!

See also: **Challenge 9: Understanding hierarchy at work and when to go around it**

                     Challenge 10: Building relationships with colleagues

                     Challenge 65: New boss

Take Action: What's your ideal job? It's time to get clear. Write out the duties, coworkers, environment and feeling you're seeking in you new job

Challenge 9.
Understanding hierarchy at work and when to go around it

Many organizations have hierarchies and specific offices designed to provide services to employees. The organizational chart and organization policies should identify these offices and what they do.

1. I use the term "**boss**" to refer to someone who supervises you or to whom you report for work assignments and other matters. In most organizations, the person who is the boss is expected to manage the work of the employees and to be the first contact for employees who have concerns, problems, or questions.

2. The "**chain of command**" is the formal hierarchy of power and authority in an organization. Generally instructions and assignments flow down from top leadership to managers to employees and accountability flows upward.

3. Some organizations have what are called "**open door**" policies, which means that any one in your chain of command welcomes individuals to talk with them about anything that's on their mind. If you are considering doing this, you might want to first check in with a trusted colleague; some organizations do not respond well when employees actually use the open door policy!

4. Your organization likely has an **Office of Corporate Compliance**. Compliance is the process of making sure the company and its employees follow appropriate laws, regulations, standards, and ethical practices. Generally this addresses both external rules (e.g., federal employment law) and internal rules (e.g., company policy).

5. **Human Resources** offices include staffing, professional development, compensation, safety and health, benefits and wellness, and employee and labor relations. Human Resources is the place to go if you have been singled out, bullied, or harassed; if you have personal circumstances that lead to you needing to take time away from work or take medical leave; or if you have questions about benefits such as vacation time or health insurance. Remember, Human Resources are primarily there to ensure the organization is operating within the scope of employment and labor law; they are not employee advocates, but can advocate for employees if your interests align with those of the organization.

6. Larger organizations may have a **Diversity, Equity and Inclusion Office** or an **Equal Employment Opportunity** office. These offices are charged with ensuring fairness, inclusion, and equal employment opportunity for all employees and job applicants consistent with federal, state, and local policies. Generally this means that actions must be taken on the basis of merit and without regard to race, color, religion, sex (including pregnancy), age (40 or older), national origin, or disability. Yes, current U.S. law indicates age discrimination only applies to those 40 or older. You would go to this office (which might be within Human Resources) if you feel you are being discriminated against.

7. Generally, if you have a problem, you should go first to your boss. It's good to ensure your boss is not blindsided or caught unaware of something they could have remedied. If you want to talk with staff in of these offices, you should let your boss know you'll be away from the job for an appointment.

8. If your boss is the problem, you can decide to go to your boss's boss or to one of the other parts of the organization. I recommend first talking with a trusted colleague to identify where to go, as some offices identified may share information you provide with your boss.

9. Generally assume that nothing you say at work is confidential unless you are specifically told it is. Assume that what you say will get back to your boss or to other people, and ensure you present your problems and challenges as diplomatically and objectively as possible.

10. Find someone outside your organization who is solely invested in your interests so you can vent, debrief, and strategize. This could include a trusted friend, mentor outside the organization, coach, or therapist.

See also: **Challenge 2: Building your network**

Challenge 13: How to have difficult conversations

Challenge 66: Not sure where to go for help with a problem

Take Action: Find the organization chart where you work and make sure you understand what each office does. If not, start asking!

Challenge 10.
Building relationships with colleagues

You spend most of your waking life with your colleagues; it's good to get along with them! Plus, good relationships can make it easier for your ideas to be implemented, for you to get things done, and for you to advance in the organization. How do you best build relationships with colleagues while not creating problems in your work life? Read on...

1. I recommend approaching work with the positive attitude that "We're all here to get a job done, and it's easier and less stressful if we work together." Maintaining a positive attitude will also serve you well throughout life!

2. Of course it's fine to socialize with your colleagues outside of work, such as at happy hours, but be aware that what you say and do (and post on social media) may get back to other colleagues or your boss. This is especially important if you are on a management track. It's wise to maintain a sense of propriety at the cost of short-term fun to keep your long-term options open.

3. Be cautious about socializing with your boss outside of work. This depends greatly on the work context. In many organizations, an occasional all-office happy hour is fine, but any more than that might be seen as inappropriate.

4. It's important to find allies at work. Start by offering support to your colleagues when you notice they need help. This will develop trust over time. Make sure you don't ask for too much and that you help them out when you can.

5. Schedule time to nurture your relationships. Reach out to your colleagues to let them know you noticed their success, or send them a link to something you think they would like.

6. Identify your work relationship needs and strengths. What are you looking for at work and what do you have to offer? Practice asking for what you need and offering up your skillset.

7. Manage boundaries at work appropriately. Friendships can start to impact your job either because you are spending so much time together or because there is a disagreement. Either way, make sure your focus at work is on work.

8. Don't gossip. If you are having a conflict with someone, talk with them directly and don't discuss it with work friends.

9. Listen actively when you are talking with a colleague. Showing them you are attending to what they are saying and acknowledging them can help build stronger relationships.

10. Trust is critical in all relationships, including work relationships. If you mess up, fess up and work on doing better next time.

11. Praise in public, correct in private. If you have concerns about one of your colleagues' work product or approach, address that in private and not in front of others. No one likes to feel ashamed or embarrassed in front of their colleagues or boss.

12. Help others find their greatness. If you support and encourage your colleagues to achieve their potential, everyone benefits.

See also: Challenge 2: Building your network
            Challenge 16: Feel isolated
            Challenge 24: Shy/introverted

Take Action: Reach out to a colleague today and work on getting to know them better.

Challenge 11.
Social media at work

It's frustrating to walk up to a coworker and find they are checking their phone. How do you balance your desire to check social media with your obligations at work?

1. Know your organization's policies about use of social media at work. Many organizations track Internet usage on company computers. Do they allow you to check your personal email at work? Are employees allowed to send tweets or update Instagram while on the clock? All activity on company computers and phones is potentially subject to their review, so proceed accordingly.

2. Especially if you are working in an office with mostly people older than you, you may want to limit the amount of time you spend on social media at work. If you are seen on social media, the assumption will likely be that you do not have enough work.

3. Organizations may have concerns about how they are portrayed if you "tag" the organization or your coworkers, or if you post information inconsistent with the organization's values. Ask if you are not sure about the policies.

4. You may want to keep your social media separated into personal and professional venues; for example, keep LinkedIn for professional contacts, and use Instagram only for personal use (and do not follow anyone you work with on your personal accounts).

5. If you are on social media at work, don't assume content is private or will be kept private, regardless of the privacy settings you chose.

6. Never post a grievance about your workplace unless you are a) out of all other options and b) okay with losing your job. If you have a concern about your workplace, take it to your boss or other appropriate person in the organization first, not to social media.

7. Organizations may want you to post/repost certain information about company news and events. Check regarding whether this is encouraged and decide if it's something you'd like to do from your professional accounts.

8. Don't respond to any competitor or anyone posting negative information or comments about the company. Let the company's public relations handle that. If you are concerned it is not being addressed, bring it up to your boss or a more appropriate person in your organization.

9. When you change organizations, be sure to update your organizational affiliation on your social media.

10. When in doubt, look to your organization's policies or public relations for guidance.

See also: Challenge 15: Unmotivated at work
Challenge 23: Bored at work
Challenge 30: Want more visibility

Take action: Find and read your organization's policy on social media at work before you need to know.

Challenge 12.
Working through differences

Workplaces can be like families, where there is support for each other. They can also be like families in that there are lots of differences and sometimes people don't get along. Work, however, is a place where it's important to get along. You don't have to like everyone, but you do have to be respectful and diplomatic and work together. If you see yourself on the management track, this is especially important.

1. Do what you can to create a culture of diversity and inclusion by being respectful to everyone and not saying or tolerating disrespectful behavior.

2. See if your organization has a diversity office and identify how you could get involved.

3. Mentor others more junior than you, especially groups that are under-represented in senior leadership. You always have something to offer, even if only support.

4. Use pronouns and names that individuals request.

5. Understand that some people may not intend to be disrespectful and may just lack awareness or be culturally insensitive. This doesn't mean that their behavior is acceptable; only that it's important not to assume negative intent. If someone is disrespectful to you, talk with them about it, and escalate if needed.

6. Be aware that there are often stark differences by seniority and tenure at organizations; sometimes there are also ageist comments about Millennials or about younger people. Try to assume positive intent first before assuming the person is a

jerk. For example, if you keep receiving menial assignments, instead of assuming it's because you're the youngest person, talk to your boss about your ability to do more challenging work. Someone has to do the menial work, though, and if you're the most junior, it might be you until someone more junior is hired or until you move up.

7. Keep clear boundaries about violations and also choose your battles. When I was in my 20s, I had a discussion with a professor about not being taken seriously with older clients because of how I looked. She said, "Don't worry, you'll get older." (She was right even though it didn't feel good at the time; I just moved on.) Much later, an employee of mine was upset and said, "I'm old enough to be your mother." This statement was more aggressive than the earlier example, and as her supervisor, I let her know that's it's not appropriate to make comments about each other's ages.

8. Although it's important to speak your mind, sometimes it's more appropriate to observe the situation and ask questions or speak up later. For example, if there is a very senior meeting with your boss, your boss's boss, and that person's boss too, that might not be the best time to ask a question or provide an insight unless specifically requested. There are political issues at play that you might not see.

9. Be open to feedback on your own behavior if you are unintentionally disrespectful to someone.

10. Speak with a mentor or trusted colleague if you have concerns about the organization's approach to diversity.

See also: Challenge 13: How to have difficult conversations

Challenge 33: How much personal information do I share with colleagues?

Challenge 49: Colleagues are aggressive, racist, sexist, homophobic, or hostile

Take Action: Consider the ways in which each of your colleagues brings a unique strength or perspective to work. Everyone has something unique to offer.

Challenge 13.
How to have difficult conversations

At various points in this book, I suggest you talk with your boss, a trusted colleague, or a mentor about a problem. This section provides some guidance on how to have these difficult conversations in a way that is respectful while keeping curiosity open to identify how to best proceed. Keep your values and goals in mind for difficult conversations. For more information, see the classic book *Difficult Conversations: How to Discuss What Matters Most* by Douglas Stone, Bruce Patton & Sheila Heen (listed in the "For further reading" section).

1. Don't avoid difficult conversations. As Author Tim Ferris said, "A person's success in life can usually be measured by the number of uncomfortable conversations he or she is willing to have." I agree with him!

2. A good first step before a difficult conversation is to identify what the issue is and what you would like the resolution of this conversation to be. Maybe you're having a problem with a colleague and you want to discuss it with a mentor. Find a way to describe the colleague problem succinctly, and ask for what you would like from the mentor. You could say, "I'd like to hear several ways to approach this situation" or "I'd like to hear what you would do if you were me."

3. Recognize that in every conversation there is often a difference between what people think, what they say, and (if the conversation takes place in writing) what they write. Starting with you, try to track the difference between what you say and what you're thinking. Keep in mind there are often comments you may think that should not be *said* or *written* at work.

4. Consider that we all have different experiences because we focus on different things, and we interpret the same events differently based on our past experiences and our values. For example, you and your boss may differ on what is meant by a "draft" report, and you may turn in something more "drafty" than your boss wanted.

5. Approach each difficult conversation with a goal of each person getting some of what they wanted. If you approach as all-or-nothing (you get everything you wanted and they get nothing), you are much less likely to have productive conversations (or to get what you want from them) in the future.

6. Demonstrate you are trying to understand what the other person is saying. Pay attention, nod, or let them know how you are interpreting what they are saying. For example, you could say, "I want to make sure I understand. You are saying…?"

7. Blame is not generally helpful if you're looking for an answer or for a change. Try to stay away from blame and just stick to the point.

8. Be careful of taking action based on assumptions. It's often best to go into a difficult conversation with a lot of questions about the other person's behavior or intentions. If you want to share with the person the impact of their behavior on you, you could say, "When [x] happened, I assumed [y]. Is that true?" or "When you [x], it was confusing to me. Could you help me understand your intentions?"

9. You may want to practice difficult conversations with a friendly partner beforehand. Anticipate what the other person might say and practice how you might respond to various comments.

10. Consider the extent to which you let your feelings be involved in the conversation. Some people suggest all work conversations should be objective and emotionless; others (like me) believe that it's okay to let people know how you feel.

("I wanted to talk with you about yesterday's meeting. When you called me out, I felt embarrassed. Can we discuss how to do this differently next time?") It is important to not let your feelings take over, however.

11. If you get upset or angry in a conversation, you can ask for a break or suggest you continue the conversation at another time. That's a better choice than crying or yelling at someone. If you do cry or yell, ask for a break and then go back to the conversation when you're more composed.

12. Recognize that you will make mistakes – we all do. Pick yourself up, identify what you learned, and keep going.

See also: Challenge 1: Understanding your values

Challenge 12: Working through differences

Challenge 38: You feel like you are not heard

Take action: What's a conversation you've been avoiding? What's one step you can take today to address the issue?

Part II. Self-management challenges

Challenge 14.
It's hard to finish tasks

I love my to-do list! As a longtime nerd, my to-do list is divided up by the same topics as my goals list. I have work to-dos listed by project as well as items to do for my fitness and travel goals. I put all information on my list including my goals, so everything is in one place. Still, I have a few items on my to-do list that just keep coming up over and over, that I can never seem to complete or cross off. We all have times where we are blocked from completing what we think we really want to do. Here's how to address that.

1. Make a list of your tasks and commit to finishing one thing on the list today.

2. Identify whether this is a task you really need to do and whether you can trade it to someone else, delegate it, give it back, or ignore it.

3. Consider professional training or reading, such as the *Getting Things Done* book and program that provide a system for organizing and completing tasks (listed in the "For further reading" section).

4. Consider an app for tracking goals such as ToDoist, Trello, or Slack.

5. Break each task down into parts and go one step at a time.

6. Identify an accountability buddy who can check in with you on completing the tasks.

7. Make sure you understand what is required to complete the tasks. If you don't, seek out others to ask questions.

8. Set a timer for 15 minutes or a half hour or whatever time feels right for you, and commit to working for that amount of time.

9. Block off time on your calendar for starting/completing the task, the same way you would for a meeting. You may want to color-code different categories of tasks.

10. If you have a lot of work tasks that are hard for you to complete, consider whether this job is right for you or whether this is just a difficult period of time that will get better.

11. Consider whether your tasks are relevant to your goals and important for you to complete. It might make sense to delete a task if it no longer makes sense for you.

12. You may want to consider obtaining a coach who can help you through completing work. In some cases, the cost could be covered by health insurance.

13. Difficulty finishing tasks may be related to underlying feelings of anxiety, fear of failure, or that you don't deserve success. If this is a pattern that is putting your career in jeopardy, you may want to seek help from a coach or therapist.

See also: Challenge 15: Unmotivated at work
Challenge 18: Feel negative about work
Challenge 19: Easily distracted
Challenge 20: Feel overwhelmed

Take action: What's one tiny step you can take today that'll get you closer to your goals? Could that one step be repeated tomorrow as well? After enough practice, this tiny step will become a habit bringing you closer and closer to your goals.

Challenge 15.
Unmotivated at work

We all get down in the dumps and feel unmotivated sometimes. If we feel really stuck and every day feels like a slog, here are some suggestions for how to pull yourself out!

1. If you have a lot of work tasks that you are not motivated to complete, consider whether this job is right for you or whether this is just a difficult period of time that will get better.

2. Consider asking your boss for a project that is more in your area of interest or more challenging.

3. Consider taking up activities outside of work that would motivate your body or your mind and could positively affect your work motivation.

4. Make a list of your tasks and commit to finishing one thing on the list today. Experience the joy of crossing something off your list.

5. Consider if there are other aspects of work that are contributing to your lack of motivation, such as a difficult commute, challenging relationships, or feeling stuck, and address those.

6. Commit yourself to completing your work at work and not taking home projects, activities, or worries about work, even if you can only make the commitment for one day.

7. Consider whether you could take a vacation or sick day to reset. It's important to give yourself a break – or a mini-break! – every now and then.

8. Set a reward for yourself after finishing tasks, especially ones that are difficult or which take a long time.

9. Identify long-term goals and consider how these current tasks fit into those goals. Motivate yourself to finish these tasks by reminding yourself of your long-term goals.

10. You may want to consider obtaining a coach who can help you through this challenge.

11. Remember that you don't have to feel well in order to complete something. Many wonderful things in the world were done by people who didn't feel very well when they did them.

See also: Challenge 14: It's hard to finish tasks

Challenge 18: Feel negative about work

Challenge 19: Easily distracted

Challenge 20: Feel overwhelmed

Take Action: If you're feeling unmotivated, what brings you joy and energy? Make a list below that you can reference anytime your emotions get low.

Challenge 16.
Feel isolated

Feeling isolated at work can sap your energy, and in general it doesn't feel good. It can also have serious consequences if you are looking to climb the corporate ladder. It's important to have colleagues and people you can talk to both in your work area and outside it.

1. Build and strengthen relationships outside of work to ensure you have support in your life.

2. Consider intentional opportunities to build relationships at work, such as inviting a colleague to coffee, to lunch, or for a drink after work. Ensure that intentional efforts to build relationships align with your values and goals.

3. Join a club or team at work, or contribute to a fundraising or charity effort. If there is not one you are interested in, consider starting one.

4. Look into organizing a happy hour or other social activities outside of the workplace with your colleagues.

5. Talk to someone you trust outside of work for an external opinion about how to feel less isolated.

6. Consider if there are aspects of the way you present yourself that may make it hard for your colleagues to be friendly with you. Do you complain a lot or ask too many personal questions? Do you always work with your door shut?

7. Compliment other people on non-physical attributes when appropriate, such as sharing with a colleague that you appreciated their ideas in a meeting. That might help start a conversation from there.

8. Join professional organizations and, if possible, attend local or national professional conferences to meet other people in your line of work. Have a goal of meeting a certain number of people at the conference or responding to online listservs at least once a month and make a game of it. Reward yourself if you hit your goal. Make sure to follow up with them after the conference.

9. Ask your boss if there are individuals they suggest you should meet who align with your interests and career goals to discuss professional activities. Prepare for the meeting, and then send them and your boss a note of thanks afterwards.

10. Consider taking a professional development or certification class at work or in the community to meet people in your line of work.

11. You may want to consider obtaining a coach who can help you through this challenge.

See also: Challenge 2: Building your network

Challenge 10: Building relationships with colleagues

Challenge 24: Shy/introverted

Take Action: What tip will you be implementing as your new "go-to" when you being to feel isolated?

Challenge 17.
Feel like an imposter

Imposter syndrome is a nagging, persistent fear of being "found out" as not being as smart or as talented or as experienced as others. We've all felt this way before as we start to experience work success. Some of us experience it intermittently throughout our lives as we take on new activities. It's not fatal, and you can definitely take steps to address your distress.

1. Create a "life resume" that highlights important events, experiences, and accomplishments, and look at it when you are feeling down. Remind yourself of how far you've come.

2. Review your job description and the required qualifications to reassure yourself you were hired for a reason and that you do indeed possess the skills and abilities to complete the job.

3. Ask your boss for feedback on your performance and focus on what you are doing well.

4. If you're not confident about your experiences, take more chances! Look for opportunities to try new things and build your skills.

5. Identify where you feel lacking and seek guidance or training in those specific areas.

6. Identify areas of your work where you feel experienced and confident. Write these down. Remind yourself of how well you perform in those areas. In the future, if you are feeling down, pull out this list and review it.

7. Consider taking a professional development or certification class at work or in the community to meet people at your level of seniority and in your line of work.

8. Consider other times that you have felt this way, and identify successes in your life where you have tackled difficult situations and emerged competent and successful. If you can't think of any of these situations, create a challenge for yourself such as completing a project or physical activity with support from friends or volunteering at an event in your community. Completing a project unrelated to work can still help you be more confident about work and give you some encouraging, feel-good vibes.

9. Focus on the value you bring rather than on attempting to obtain perfection in what you're doing. Remember that perfection can often hurt you in the long run, especially if it keeps you from finishing work now.

10. Talk to someone you trust outside of work for an outside opinion.

11. You may want to consider obtaining a coach who can help you through this challenge.

12. "Fake it till you make it." Many times acting confident can help you feel more confident.

13. Remember you can *give* your best without having to *be* the best.

See also: **Challenge 1: Understanding your values**

                     Challenge 3: Setting goals and priorities

                     Challenge 26: Difficult to accept praise

Take Action: Take a moment to look back and reflect on your life. What are you most proud of? Take notice of how far you've come and all the things you've learned. Write some accomplishments down below so you will remember. Don't be so hard on yourself -- you're doing great!

Challenge 18.
Feel negative about work

Most of us have moments where we really dislike our job. We start to complain and gripe and scowl, and pretty soon everyone can tell we're unhappy. It's okay to be unhappy sometimes, but persistent negativity can lead colleagues to not want to work with us and be detrimental to our careers. It doesn't have to be that way!

1. Write down at least five things about work you feel positive about.

2. Identify one area that you feel negative about and challenge yourself to come up with 10 ways to make it better. For example, if you feel negative about a high workload, maybe you come up with silly ideas, like arranging a lunch break where you and your colleagues can talk about something other than work or suggest each person choose a song to play at the top of the hour. You could also come up with some serious ideas, like asking the boss for help managing the workload, or working with your colleagues to streamline tasks.

3. Consider how you can address the issues you feel negative about. What can you to do address them? How can you turn the negative into a positive? For example, if you feel resentful at a situation you think is unfair, talk to people about your perceived unfairness and try to make it more fair.

4. Consider your environment: if you are always around complainers, stop spending time with them or stop the complaining by saying, "There's so much else going on. Let's talk about [something positive]."

5. Choose to spend time with positive people in the office and outside of work. Building positive relationships will help you feel more positive about work.

6. Limit out-of-work complaining about work to 10 minutes or less per day.

7. Consider limiting time outside of work with colleagues if the discussions center around work unless you are actively engaged in activities (e.g., ballgame, charity) or unless you can limit negative conversations and complaining.

8. Do not contribute to complaining or gossip. You can use neutral statements like "Huh" or "I don't see it that way" or "I'd rather discuss something else. What about...?"

9. If you can't shake your negativity, try to identify what the negativity is about: the company, the mission, the job, your colleagues? Consider if this is the right job for you and how you could take steps to make things better.

10. Talk to someone you trust outside of work for an outside opinion.

11. Update your resume to reflect your recent accomplishments. If you are having trouble thinking of any, identify goals you can pursue and create accomplishments you will have in several months.

12. You may want to consider obtaining a coach who can help you through this challenge.

See also: Challenge 15: Unmotivated at work

Challenge 19: Easily distracted

Challenge 20: Feel overwhelmed

Challenge 40: Meetings are frustrating

Take Action: When you're in the middle of office "water-cooler talk," how will you respond? How can you be the person that always sees positive in your work situation?

Challenge 19.
Easily distracted

We can sometimes lose our ... um ... train of ... thought, especially when we are stressed or overwhelmed. It's okay! Here are steps to help you get back on track.

1. Reduce clutter in your work area by making your work area a clutter-free zone, even when you're not using it. Keeping your work area clean can keep you from being distracted by it.

2. Reduce additional distractions by spending some time in another work area, such as an empty conference room or the library if possible.

3. Wear headphones if that helps you focus, if your work situation allows.

4. Make a list of your tasks and commit to finishing one thing on the list today. Experience the joy of crossing something off your list!

5. Consider coming in early or staying late to have uninterrupted time to work before or after your colleagues are there.

6. Turn off email notifications, and limit checking email and Internet time to a few set times a day when you are working on an important or time-sensitive project.

7. Give yourself blocks of "focus time" to work on specific projects. Set time on your calendar to work on each of your tasks so you have dedicated time to multiple tasks over the course of the day.

8. Turn off phone alerts and eliminate the temptation of social media at work if possible.

9. Give yourself a break and spend your lunch or break time talking with others, reviewing social media, taking a walk, or anything else you enjoy so you can go back and be focused.

10. Consider if your diet is affecting you, such as too much caffeine or sugar.

11. Consider whether you should talk with a therapist or physician about your distractibility issues if they feel severe.

12. If you can, close your door or put up a sign asking people to respect your privacy because you're working on a project.

See also: Challenge 3: Setting goals and priorities
            Challenge 14: It's hard to finish tasks
            Challenge 20: Feel overwhelmed

Take Action: Which one of these tips stuck out the most? How can you take action on it this week? Make a plan and stick to it.

Challenge 20.
Feel overwhelmed

Sometimes it happens that we just can't keep up! If everything keeps coming at us without a break, we can get completely overwhelmed. Communicating your needs and collaborating with others on how to ensure the most important things done is a way through this challenge.

1. Periodically during the day, stop and take a deep breath, stand, and stretch. Take a short walk outside of your work space if possible. Build in regular breaks during the day to walk or meditate and clear your head. Even five minutes can be an important "reset" to help lower your stress.

2. Talk with your boss to clarify their priorities for your tasks so you can focus on them accordingly.

3. Ask for more time if possible. If enough time hasn't been allotted to finish a task or project, it's not surprising that you're feeling overwhelmed. It's more responsible to ask for more time than to deliver poor or sloppy work product because you didn't have enough time.

4. Share with your boss that you are feeling overwhelmed with the amount of work and ask for assistance in how to manage the workload, temporary assistance to complete tasks, or strategies to work more efficiently.

5. Develop mantras that you can say to yourself or program in your phone (such as setting affirmations using your phone alarms or an app such as MindJogger) to repeat during the day that will help you feel less frantic. For example, "You can do this!" or "One thing at a time."

6. Talk to someone you trust outside of work for an external opinion about how to feel less frantic.

7. Consider whether you may be doing work that isn't yours. Sometimes we pick up the work of others because we're good at it or because we are perfectionists. If you find yourself taking on tasks that aren't yours, talk with your boss about it or figure out how to reallocate those tasks.

8. If there are repetitive tasks or tasks that take a long time, ask around to identify ways to do them more efficiently.

9. Identify people who seem calm and ask them what they do to stay calm in stressful situations.

10. Consider starting a meditation or yoga practice.

11. Consider whether you can take something off your to-do list, or at least delay it.

12. Consider delegating tasks if at all possible. You will still be responsible for their completion, but at least you can focus on other things for a little while as someone else slogs through the details. Delegating also gives you the opportunity to help someone more junior and practice your mentoring skills.

13. You may want to consider obtaining a coach or occupational therapist who can help you prioritize tasks and reduce your feelings of being overwhelmed.

See also: Challenge 3: Setting goals and priorities

Challenge 18: Feel negative about work

Challenge 61: Don't have resources to complete work

Challenge 62: Your boss has unreasonable expectations

Take Action: What's your favorite mantra to help keep you motivated? Write it below and consider sticking it on a post-it note you can see each day.

Challenge 21.
Want to improve time management/ organization

Having a "system" for managing our time, priorities, and resources can make our work life so much easier – but for many of us, it's a challenge to set it up. If you struggle with organizing your time, here are options to help you figure it out.

1. Consider professional training and books, such as the *Getting Things Done* program that provides a system for organizing and completing tasks. (listed in the "For further reading" section).

2. Make a list of everything that needs to be done, prioritize, and commit to completing the first item on the list.

3. If you feel like you don't have enough time, consider that you are not prioritizing the time you do have.

4. Ask for help if you are not sure how work assignments should be prioritized. Your boss should be able to help you understand their priorities so that you can make choices.

5. If you have multiple bosses who are each acting as if you have a full-time job with only them, ask to meet with all of them together to work out your priorities across groups. Share your current list of activities and ask for feedback on how to ensure each group gets what it needs.

6. Make a list of what meetings you attend and projects on your plate, and consider the value of each regarding how much they are helpful to achieve goals and priorities. Consider discussing with your staff or your boss to identify which meetings could be improved, which you can delegate, and which you can no longer attend.

7. Identify someone who seems very organized and ask them for some pointers and tips.

8. Be aware that ways of keeping yourself organized may change over time.

9. If you have the option to delegate or trade activities that are not your strengths, such as scheduling or making to-do lists, find others who can help you. Try to play to your strengths as much as possible.

10. Talk to someone you trust outside of work for an outside opinion.

11. You may want to consider obtaining a coach who can help you with time management and organization.

See also: Challenge 3: Setting goals and priorities

Challenge 5: How to obtain a career coach

Challenge 20: Feel overwhelmed

Take Action: What's keeping you from being organized? What's one thing you can do to be more organized in your work and world?

Challenge 22.
Difficulty saying no

Saying no at work can be a tricky subject. Sometimes we want to say no because we don't want to do it, we don't think we should be asked to do it, or it's just too much. On the other hand, we are being paid to do a job and don't want to harm our professional relationships or reputation by saying "no" too much. Here are some suggestions for when and how to say no.

1. If you think you might want to say no, ask for time to think about it. A good phrase to use is, "When do you need an answer?"

2. Identify if this is an activity that you can legitimately decline. Most work tasks should just be completed as asked, and save the "nos" for important situations.

3. "No" might be appropriate if: the work is outside of the scope of your job, you feel the work is unsafe or inappropriate, or you will not be able to complete the work on time and with sufficient quality.

4. Consider whether you can offer an alternative instead of saying no. For example, you could say, "I'm happy to help with that project but I'm booked this week. Could we discuss it next week?" or "I'm not able to do all of that now, but I could help with part of it. Would that work?"

5. If you are asked at work to attend a non-work event, such as a party, you don't need to provide an explanation. In fact, it's often better to just say no instead of explaining ("I have a date that night"; "My sister is in town"), because your explanations

might lead the other person to feel it's okay to try to bargain with you ("Bring your sister!").

6. If your difficulty saying no is affecting your work, you can talk with your boss about helping you. For example, you can arrange with your boss that when someone asks you to do something, you'll let them know you have to check in with your boss. That will give you some time to discuss with your boss and figure out how to best respond.

7. If your colleagues are aware of a goal (or perhaps if they're not), you can let them know you are working on a goal and can't take on anything else. You could say, "I'm spending the next two weeks on this report, so I can't take anything on right now."

8. If you say no to someone and they get angry, it doesn't necessarily mean you should have said yes. It means there are issues on their side. Ideally the other person can have a reasonable conversation with you about the issue.

9. If you're not the right person for the job, you could suggest someone else, especially if this is a good opportunity for a colleague.

10. If there are certain activities you want to always decline, such as data entry or after-hours socializing with colleagues, keep a note of those in your personal notes. If someone asks you to do one of those tasks, you can say "no" or you could say, "I'm no longer doing data entry. You could ask [other person who does data entry]."

11. If someone is asking you to do something illegal or unethical, or if you feel unsafe saying no, attempt to get out of the situation and seek consultation from your boss or a trusted colleague.

See also: Challenge 3: Setting goals and priorities

Challenge 13: How to have difficult conversations

Challenge 25: Overly concerned or underconcerned about others' feelings

Challenge 55. Boss asks me to do work outside of official duties

Take Action: What's something you need to say 'no' to? What's stopping you? Knowing what you know now, how can you approach the situation differently next time it comes up?

Challenge 23.
Bored at work

After we figure out how to do our jobs and get used to the ebb and flow of work cycles, sometimes we can feel like we're just doing the same thing over and over and can get bored. This doesn't have to be a problem – being bored is one of the easiest problems to solve!

1. If you find yourself frequently bored at work, consider whether this is the right job for you. If it's not, start taking steps to figure out a better fit in the same company or somewhere else.

2. Review your list of goals and identify what you can work on while you're bored. Perhaps you can listen to a podcast when you are doing dull work?

3. Confide in someone you trust outside of work and ask for their opinion.

4. Create challenges for yourself at work. For example, when I worked as a writer, we would challenge each other to include a specific word in an assignment. The winner put a random type of fabric in an article about baseball.

5. Ask your boss for a challenging assignment that will stretch your skills.

6. Remind yourself of your long-term goals and how the current activities fit into those long-term goals. If they don't, then reassess. If you don't have long-term goals, create them.

7. Talk with your boss about your work duties and how they are contributing to the company. Ask for suggestions to challenge you more.

8. Consider choosing to approach work with a sense of excitement and joy. Make a game of it if you have to!

9. Schedule meetings with other teams/departments within your organization so you can identify and understand what projects they are working on. Use this information to discuss with your boss how you could contribute.

10. Create excitement for yourself outside of work by engaging in adventurous physical activities or whatever would help you experience fun and energy. An inspiring evening of a movie, play, live music, or dinner with friends can put you in a great mood the next day, even at work.

11. Consider setting stretch goals for yourself by setting goals that require you to really work for them. This could be increasing your speed, accuracy, knowledge, or something else. For example, when I was on kitchen duty in the military and had stacks of eggs to crack (a dull, boring task if there was one), I took the opportunity to learn how to crack eggs one-handed. After all that practice, I became quite good at it, and it's a skill I still have!

See also: Challenge 3: Setting goals and priorities
Challenge 14: It's hard to finish tasks
Challenge 15: Unmotivated at work

Take Action: What's a new topic/task/challenge you'd like to take on at work? What's in it for you? What's in it for your company?

Challenge 24.
Shy/Introverted

At least half of the U.S. population is introverted, which describes someone who is predominantly focused on their own thoughts and feelings rather than on externalities. People who are introverted sometimes are less comfortable in large groups of people and feel more energized by time alone. Extroverts, on the other hand, find energy from interaction with others. In addition, many of us are shy in work environments, especially where we may feel like the youngest person in the company. It can be hard to be an introvert in a world that seems like it rewards more outgoing people!

1. Read *Quiet: The Power of Introverts in a World that Can't Stop Talking* by Susan Cain or listen to her TED Talk on the topic to consider how introverts contribute to the world in unique ways (details listed in the "For further reading" section).

2. Consider how you feel shyness holds you back – in developing relationships, speaking up, or something else? – and find ways to work on increasing your skills and comfort in this area.

3. Identify other people at work who seem shy and build relationships with them. Ask them how they approach their work, especially aspects that require you to be more outgoing.

4. Practice speaking up. Every day, commit to a goal of saying hello to one new person. After a few weeks, commit to starting a conversation, and then asking someone to have coffee. Commit to speaking up in a meeting, even if just to agree and confirm that you liked or support someone's idea.

5. Set up meetings to get a chance to talk with people and ask them questions. Sometimes it's easier to talk to someone if we

view it as a work requirement instead of as our own initiative. It's also good to provide people with time to think about decisions rather than insisting they are made in the meeting itself. Some people work best when not put on the spot.

6. Use email to express your ideas if you are more comfortable writing instead of talking.

7. If you are uncomfortable with people stopping by your office or cubicle to chat, put up a sign for a few hours a day that says do not disturb or you are working on a project.

8. It may be possible to trade some duties with a colleague who is more outgoing.

9. If you are in a job that requires a lot of communication that makes you uncomfortable, consider whether this might not be the right job for you.

10. If you are painfully shy, you may want to consider obtaining help from a coach or therapist who can assist you with this challenge.

See also: Challenge 10: Building relationships with colleagues

Challenge 17: Feel like an imposter

Challenge 25: Overly concerned or underconcerned about others' feelings

Take Action: Do you identify with being an introvert? Which tip feels the best to start implementing?

Challenge 25.
Overly concerned or unconcerned about others' feelings

Sometimes we are so concerned about others' feelings that we find ourselves apologizing frequently, thanking people profusely, or not being direct or honest because we don't want to be hurtful. If this sounds like you, read on to find ways to balance so that you can be forthright and kind at the same time (without apologizing or being a jerk!).

1. When someone brings a problem to you, train yourself to first ask yourself "Whose problem is this?" Make sure it's your problem before you try to help them solve the problem. (Sometimes people try to make *their* problems *your* problems.)

2. As you are starting to improve your sensitivity to others' feelings, you can start a conversation by saying, "I want to talk about something but I'm not sure how to say it...." Most times people will let you know that what you said sounded just fine. Note this is a temporary solution, not a long-term one.

3. Identify your own feelings in a given situation and remind yourself that your feelings are valid. If you tend to be unconcerned about others, this may be a challenging task.

4. If you find yourself always deferring to others or apologizing, or if you are not sensitive enough to other people's feelings, let a trusted colleague know you are trying to improve and ask that person to help you identify when you may not realize you're doing the behavior. Being accountable to someone else can help you change your behavior more quickly. For example, you can say, "I am working on balancing being direct and honest with being sensitive and respectful. Please let me know

if I say or do something that makes you feel disrespected and how I could improve an interaction like this in the future."

5. Be aware that it's hard to understand other people's feelings, and where to draw the line in our efforts to communicate. Keep practicing, note when you do well or not well, and keep improving!

6. Talk to someone you trust outside of work for an external opinion.

7. Limit yourself to one thank you per interaction. It's important to appreciate others' generosity, but being overly solicitous can be off-putting. If you don't tend to say 'thank you' in conversations with colleagues, start now.

8. Remember that each of us is responsible for our own feelings. Even if you feel responsible, or if someone tries to make you responsible, ultimately each of us carries our own responsibility.

9. If you find you're not saying what you mean because you're afraid you'll hurt others' feelings, run your comments by a trusted colleague or friend outside of work to get honest feedback.

10. If this is an ongoing or severe problem, you may want to consider obtaining a therapist or coach who can help you through this challenge.

See also: Challenge 4: When and how to obtain a mentor

Challenge 10: Building relationships with colleagues

Challenge 22: Difficulty saying no at work

Challenge 24: Shy/introverted

Take Action: List out your trusted advisors you can lean on for support when these feelings come up.

Challenge 26.
Difficult to accept praise

Have you ever seen someone who is uncomfortable accepting praise? They blush, stammer, look away, minimize their role, or deflect the feedback; this often makes the person giving praise uncomfortable too. If this is you, read on.

1. If you don't already, start complimenting colleagues so you get more comfortable giving compliments. Make sure your compliments are sincere and not focused on their physical appearance. Make a point to compliment a few people every day. Some of those people will compliment you back, which will help you learn to respond more positively. (It also helps to build more positive relationships and stay positive in the workplace.)

2. At work and outside of work, practice saying "Thank you" when anyone gives you a compliment. No need to say anything else; just "thank you."

3. Notice how other people respond to compliments and consider how you want to respond.

4. Identify someone who is good at accepting praise and model after them.

5. Be sure to repay compliments to others.

6. Keep it sincere.

7. Talk to someone you trust outside of work for an external opinion on how you react to praise and how it makes them feel.

8. If you have a physical reaction to compliments, such as blushing, try to find the humor in it or even comment on it.

9. Respond to the compliment with a comment in kind; for example, if someone praises your report say, "Thanks! I was really proud of completing it on time."

10. Don't minimize the praise by saying something like, "It wasn't difficult."

11. Use praise as an avenue to get to the next thing you want. Say, "Thanks! I'm glad you noticed, because I would like to do more work in that arena. Do you know of any opportunities?"

12. Consider turning praise into a reference opportunity for LinkedIn or your resume by following up in an email.

See also: Challenge 10: Building relationships with colleagues

Challenge 17: Feel like an imposter

Challenge 29: Want feedback on work performance

Take Action: How will you train yourself to receive compliments graciously?

Challenge 27.
Hard to make small talk

Everyone has to make small talk at some point. You can stick to talking about the weather or you can work on it more and open up new possibilities.

1. If you think small talk is dull and pointless, change your perspective. If you go into situations or conversations believing you will find someone interesting, learn something new, or make a new connection, you will find it much easier to engage with others.

2. Be prepared with a few questions or conversation starters before going into a situation that might require small talk. For example, you can start work small talk by saying, "Tell me about what you do at your company." Make sure to smile.

3. Identify people who seem very skilled at making small talk and ask them how they do it, or simply observe them in action.

4. Google "small talk" to find websites with lists of "small talk" questions.

5. Skim publications, news, and websites from your field so you can bring up an idea from something you reviewed.

6. Ask people about TV, movies, sports, or other easy topics within pop culture. You can connect with them without the risk of feeling intimidated/inadequate from talking about work. If you don't know about a movie, for example, ask them to explain it to you or why they liked it so much.

7. Create an "elevator speech" (a three-sentence description of what you do) so that when you are asked about your work, you

can respond confidently. Consider creating another one for what you like to do outside of work.

8. Practice small talk with a friend or colleague so it becomes natural. Everything is harder when it's not a habit.

9. Read the book *How to Talk to Anyone: 92 Little Tricks for Big Success in Relationships* by Leil Lowndes (details listed in the "For further reading" section).

10. Ask people what they do *outside* of work. You might be surprised!

11. When you go to a professional or social event, commit to introducing yourself to at least five people. Practice!

12. Tell a colleague you trust that you are working on improving your small talk game and ask them to provide you with feedback whenever they notice you doing well or not well in small talk.

13. Toastmasters helps people improve their comfort speaking in public, including impromptu speaking. Find a Toastmasters group in your area and start going to meetings.

14. Talk to someone you trust outside of work for an outside opinion on how to make better small talk.

See also: Challenge 10: Building relationships with colleagues

Challenge 24: Shy/introverted

Challenge 28: Difficulty speaking in public/giving presentations

Challenge 33: How much personal information do I share with colleagues?

Take Action: Write out your elevator pitch below so you can reference at anytime.

Challenge 28.
Difficulty speaking in public/giving presentations

Public speaking is the top fear of humans – often more terrifying than the fear of dying! Learning to speak well in public is an important skill that will serve you well not just at work, but throughout your life.

1. Toastmasters is an international organization that helps people improve their public speaking in a safe and friendly environment. Find a Toastmasters group in your area and start going to meetings.

2. Volunteer for an opportunity to speak publicly, and practice at home and in front of friends until you get it the way you want it.

3. Ask for specific feedback on your public speaking. You may want to ask for feedback about your speech, word choice, tone, vocal variety, and how you use your body during the speech.

4. When preparing a speech early in your speaking career, plan to make three points; tell the audience your topic, tell them the three points, expanding on each one; and then summarize.

5. Using your phone's camera or speaker, record yourself giving the speech ahead of time. You can identify issues with timing, tone, or excessive "likes" and "umms" to work on.

6. Consider what your "Call to Action" is for your speech: What is it you want your audience to think, feel, or do differently after your speech?

7. Identify your pre-speaking anxiety spikes and plan for them. I always need to go to the restroom one more time before speaking in public. Other people fear a dry throat, so they

bring water or lozenges. Whatever your fear is, instead of trying to eliminate it, plan around it.

8. Practice speaking up in small meetings, then in larger meetings. Recognize that it's brave to speak up and reward yourself for doing so.

9. Work on your tone of voice and confidence by over-preparing if you need to. Practice using different levels of preparation – word for word, an outline with bullets, just a main outline, entire speech memorized – until you find a sweet spot that works for you.

10. If your public speaking tends to involve a question and answer period, anticipate what questions you might be asked and draft answers to them. Also, it's okay to say, "That's a good question," as it give you a few seconds to prepare your answer.

11. When you start a speech, keep going! Even if you lose your train of thought or stammer, take a breath, find your place, and start again. Pushing yourself to continue will make you a better speaker.

12. Identify someone who seems comfortable speaking in public and ask them how they do it.

13. You may want to consider working with a partner to prepare and give a short practice talk in front of just each other.

See also: Challenge 17: Feel like an imposter

Challenge 27: Hard to make small talk

Challenge 30: Want more visibility

Challenge 38: You feel like you are not heard

Search youtube for 'inspirational public speaking.' You'll find both excellent speakers and plenty of inspiration to up your public speaking game!

Challenge 29.
Want feedback on work performance

Some bosses are generous with feedback, and others don't provide much feedback at all. Sometimes people have good intentions or provide feedback that is delivered in a very clumsy or even hurtful way. Others use the guise of "providing feedback" to say things that aren't helpful at all. The best way to learn how to ask for and receive feedback is to practice. If you're not getting feedback on how to improve, learn to ask for it.

1. Schedule a time to talk with your boss to ask for feedback. Have a list of your projects and three-, six-, and nine-month goals ready for your boss to reflect upon. Ideally, you can send your brief list to your boss so they are prepared.

2. Ask a trusted friend or mentor for feedback based on what they know about you. Make sure you aren't asking friends who will only give you positive feedback. While everyone needs a confidence boost, it promotes growth to receive and build upon constructive criticism.

3. If you don't want feedback on your work performance, consider why you don't. None of us are perfect; however, obtaining feedback can help us improve for this job or for the next job.

4. If someone has stopped giving you feedback, consider how you accept feedback. It's important to be able to accept feedback gracefully and ask clarifying questions without being defensive.

5. You might be apprehensive about receiving feedback, but it's rarely as bad as we think. If you approach the situation as an opportunity to learn and grow, it will be much easier. If you

receive difficult feedback, you may want to discuss with a close friend or colleague. It's okay to vent a little (outside of work) but then focus on what there is to learn from the feedback.

6. Take notes about your daily activities to identify what went well and not as well in your daily work activities. After a few weeks, review the notes to identify patterns with specific projects, interactions, or people who are more challenging for you.

7. When asking for feedback, keep your language simple: "Can you give me some suggestions about what I'm doing well and what I could do better?"

8. Consider asking specific questions after completion of a substantial project, such as, "Could we take some time to discuss what went well and what didn't go as well on that project now that we're finished?"

9. Identify someone who is highly skilled in an area you want to improve, and ask them how they do it. Also ask them for feedback!

10. Remember, your peers can be valuable sources of feedback. Ask them for observations on how you're handling situations. This is especially helpful if you can tell a trusted colleague that you're working on improving a certain aspect of your performance and would appreciate their feedback.

11. Integrate feedback into your goals so that you can make a point to learn more about the skill you want to improve, take chances to practice the skill, and get feedback again.

12. Remember that it's better to receive feedback during the year rather than being surprised by it during an annual performance review. Maintain a folder in which you store your notes, critiques, and accomplishments through the performance year. This will help you when writing a self-review.

13. Make sure that when people provide you with feedback that you receive it graciously. It's okay to ask a few clarifying questions, but don't badger the feedback provider or argue with them about their perspective, or they'll be unlikely to provide feedback in the future.

See also: Challenge 3: Setting goals and priorities

Challenge 4: When and how to obtain a mentor

Challenge 13: How to have difficult conversations

Challenge 34: Asking for a letter of recommendation

Take Action: What is one step you can take to obtain feedback?

Challenge 30.
Want more visibility

Feeling invisible? Sometimes it feels like we work our tails off and no one is seeing our accomplishments. Do not despair! Increasing visibility is very do-able.

1. Understand why you would like visibility: Because you want a promotion? Because you want a raise? Because you feel like you are not being acknowledged? Consider additional ways to achieve that goal.

2. Consider what having more visibility would look like for you and whether those are reasonable expectations for someone at your level of seniority in the field. Consult with a trusted colleague if you are not sure.

3. Consider what you will do when you have the visibility you want. It can be a blessing and a curse. Once you have eyes on you, are you prepared to maintain the momentum?

4. Remember you are responsible for your visibility and your career. Do your own homework and outreach to ensure you are obtaining the level of influence you would like.

5. Observe others in your organization to understand how they promote themselves or promote others in ways that increase their visibility. Are there meetings in which workers' achievements are announced? A newsletter? Ask someone who was recently praised how it came about that they were featured.

6. Identify specific accomplishments you would like more visibility on and ask your boss or a trusted colleague about

how to get more visibility.

7. Join a professional organization associated with your field to observe how others achieve visibility.

8. When beginning a significant project, talk with your boss about how you both will share it with others at your company or outside your company.

9. Identify if it is appropriate to write an article about your accomplishment for a professional association magazine or newsletter or for the company's newsletter.

10. Consider your own role in promoting an environment for recognition and visibility in your organization (shout-out boxes, meeting announcements, etc.).

11. Do the work to deserve visibility. Do noteworthy things so that people will want to talk about how wonderful you are.

12. Consider ways to increase your visibility, such as on your company's intranet or by blogging. Remember to be positive on public forums so that your visibility will have the intended effect of promoting your skills at work. Confirm your company's rules on whether and how you can identify yourself as affiliated with the company on non-official communications.

13. Have an informal conversation with your company's Public Relations office about your interests in visibility. Check with your boss about how to approach them if you're not sure, but they may be open to having a brief phone or in-person conversation about what they do and how they help bring visibility to the company (and possibly you!).

14. You may want to consider obtaining a coach who can help you through this challenge.

See also: Challenge 2: Social media at work

Challenge 31: Want to increase influence

Challenge 38: You feel like you are not heard

Challenge 51: Boss takes credit for your work

Take Action: What are two ways can you gain more visibility?

Challenge 31.
Want to increase influence

You have great ideas, but they're not getting heard. How can you increase your influence and make it likely that people will hear you?

1. Observe others in your organization to understand how they increase their own influence and the influence of others.

2. Read Robert Cialdini's *Influence* and *Influence Without Authority* by Allan Cohen and David Bradford. Both have excellent insight and specific strategies that can help you be successful.

3. Attend a leadership seminar in your field, a general leadership seminar, or a program like Toastmasters that helps teach leadership skills.

4. Talk to someone you trust outside of work for an outside opinion on how to increase your influence.

5. Self-reflect on your communication style. The way you communicate may be off-putting to others or may not reflect the way you are intending.

6. Identify specifically what you want and work on achieving those specific goals.

7. Work on improving your public speaking, as clear, confident speakers are more likely to be seen as influencers.

8. Continue to build relationships as you work on increasing your influence. Positive relationships are influence multipliers.

9. Consider dressing for the job you want, not the job you have. Depending on your organization and field, dressing up may increase your influence.

10. Consider building mentoring or collegial relationships with people who have influence. As you get to know them, you can learn from how they wield influence.

11. You may want to consider obtaining a coach who can help you strategize how to increase your influence.

12. Remember you are responsible for your influence and your career. Do your own homework and outreach to ensure you are obtaining the level of influence you would like.

See also: Challenge 2: Building your network

Challenge 30: Want more visibility

Challenge 38: You feel like you are not heard

Take Action: Want 1:1 support for increasing your influence in a way that feels good to you? Reach out to me at www.leadwithwisdom.com.

Challenge 32.
Office romance from crush to breakup

Many people swear against office romances, and plenty others meet their significant other in the workplace. Whatever you choose to do, be aware of the risks and be professional. Trust me, take the long view on this one.

1. You generally get one chance for an office romance. If you have more than one romance in the same office, you may not like how you begin to be perceived.

2. Be aware of your organization's policies about office relationships. Many organizations forbid relationships between supervisors and supervisees; others require you to inform your supervisor of your relationship. Know the rules before you get started.

3. Ask yourself if you would be willing to leave your job if things became uncomfortable, such as if you break up.

4. Never engage in public displays of affection at work with a colleague. No holding hands, no kissing, no nothing. It will not be helpful for you.

5. If you work with the other person, consider transferring out of your position before you start dating.

6. If you are friends with your colleagues on social media, be wary of what you post with regard to your office romance.

7. Some people have very sensitive antennae to pick up on flirting. Others may be biased against women or have views of women's sexuality that are not consistent with your values (e.g., shaming women who are sexual; praising men who are).

If you are flirting with someone, be aware that others may be noticing. Better to keep flirting outside of work.

8. If your organization is very conservative, be especially careful of office romances, as they may be viewed more negatively than in less-conservative workplaces.

9. Hopefully this is a thing of the past, but if an office romance also means coming out, be aware of office politics or sensitivities related to LGBT issues. If your organization or its employees are not supportive of you coming out, consider whether this is the right organization for you.

10. If your office romance is going well and you would like to let people at work know about your relationship, keep announcements low-key unless you are announcing an engagement. Be prepared to address any direct or indirect concerns about favoritism.

See also: Challenge 1: Understanding your values

Challenge 13: How to have difficult conversations

Challenge 16: Feel isolated

Challenge 22: Difficulty saying no

Take Action: Look up your office policies on office relationships so you're clear before any crushes start.

Challenge 33.
How much personal information do I share with colleagues?

Some offices are very professional where no one knows about each other's personal lives, whereas others are full of people who want to know all about you. Especially when there are parts of your life outside of work you don't want to share, knowing how much to share is critical.

1. You don't have to share anything you don't want to share, including your partner or parent status, religion, sexual orientation, or even what you do on the weekends.

2. Before you share information about yourself, notice how much personal information your colleagues share with each other. Also notice what colleagues do with personal information they receive. If you hear people discussing personal information later on, you may want to reconsider disclosing personal information to them.

3. Consider not immediately connecting with colleagues on social media until you get to know them better and also keeping your social media set to private. It's okay to let people know if asked that you don't connect with work colleagues on social media, or that you connect with work colleagues only through professional media such as LinkedIn.

4. Talk to someone you trust outside of work for an outside opinion regarding specific information you are considering sharing at work.

5. Consider how to continue to build relationships without sharing information you don't feel comfortable sharing. For example, you can find neutral topics of mutual interest that you can discuss with your colleagues.

6. Observe what happens when people share things about themselves at work, especially personal attributes you share.

7. Identify what topics you always want to keep off limits, which may include politics, religion, medical issues, and sex, and make sure you don't talk about them.

8. Start sharing small on a topic that is not stressful for you. For example, share about an activity you did the past weekend without sharing details about your personal relationships. Start small and then proceed by gauging others' reactions and how comfortable you are with the sharing.

9. If there's a sensitive topic that you're not sure will be received well (e.g., sexual orientation, religion), first question if you should share, and why you are considering sharing. Then consider asking someone at work who will likely be sensitive to that specific topic for ideas about how much they share with others.

10. If you feel you have over-shared, ask a trusted colleague for their feedback and how to address it. And make sure you don't do it again.

11. Consider using the grapevine to your advantage. If you have something you need to share but don't want to personally tell people, intentionally share it with the office gossip. If you know that person will share with everyone, plan it carefully and know that the information will get out.

See also: Challenge 1: Understanding your values

Challenge 10: Building relationships with colleagues

Challenge 22: Difficulty saying no

Challenge 25: Overly concerned or underconcerned about others' feelings

Take Action: What topics are not open for discussion? What topics are open? Get clear here before you're in a sharing situation.

Challenge 34.
Asking for a letter of recommendation

Asking for a letter of recommendation can be nerve-wracking. Sometimes we don't want to know what the boss really thinks of us. Sometimes we don't want to add more work to the boss's plate, and sometimes we are just uncomfortable with compliments. Not a problem! You can do this.

1. Do your best to have a positive relationship with your boss that includes asking them for feedback occasionally (or at least more than an annual, required performance review). Getting a letter of recommendation isn't impossible when you don't have a great relationship, but it's easier if you do.

2. Let your boss know why you are requesting a letter, whether for another job or for an academic program. Let them know if there are ways the academic program will benefit them; for example, you could say, "I want to take an accounting graduate program because it will help me conduct our analyses much better." Be specific.

3. If the letter is for another job, first discuss your leaving, then request a letter. Thank the boss for the opportunity to work together, explain why you're leaving, give a reasonable timeline, and then ask for a letter of recommendation.

4. Make it as easy as possible for your boss to complete the letter of recommendation. Provide a copy of any forms, your resume, and any other information that is needed. Be very clear on the letter's due date.

5. You may want to offer to provide some "talking points" to emphasize what you would appreciate the boss focusing on in the letter.

6. Your boss may ask you to draft a letter. Don't be offended! Write a letter that speaks directly to the criteria stated in the letter request, and send to the boss with a statement like, "Thanks so much for writing a recommendation! I drafted a letter for your review. Please feel free to edit as you wish." The worst case is that they will accept your letter as is, so make sure it's good.

7. Be careful of using "grindstone adjectives." These are words that focus on your effort (e.g., hard worker) instead of your ability (e.g., brilliant). Studies demonstrate letters of recommendation for women tend to use grindstone adjectives more than letters for men, suggesting that women try hard but men have ability.

8. Offer to discuss the letter with your boss if they do not want you to draft a letter or give talking points.

9. Keep a copy of the letter if possible. It will be helpful for the next letter of recommendation you need. You can use it as a start and update or embellish as needed for the new opportunity!

10. Most letters start with an introduction paragraph about what the letter is about and how the writer knows the applicant. For example, "I am writing to provide my strongest recommendation for Alex Smith to enroll in your Master's program in Journalism. I have known Alex for two years; Alex is a staff writer at the Times, where I am an editor."

11. End letters of recommendation with a closing statement indicating strong approval for the applicant and an offer to contact. For example, "In sum, Alex has my highest

recommendation. Please contact me at [xx] if I can be of further assistance. You will be proud to call them a graduate."

See also: Challenge 3: Setting goals and priorities

Challenge 10: Building relationships with colleagues

Challenge 13: How to have difficult conversations

Challenge 26: Difficult to accept praise

Take Action: Draft a letter of recommendation you would love someone to write for you. Identify what you want to have accomplished in the next year or two that someone could brag about you and work to achieve those accomplishments.

Challenge 35.
Asking for a raise

We all want to get paid more, but raises often seem elusive. Asking your boss for a raise is one of the most stressful conversations to have. But you can do it and be successful!

1. Proactively communicate accomplishments to your boss over time so that they have a sense of the good work you have been doing.

2. First be sure you deserve a raise and that you can document your accomplishments. Gather your evidence, keeping in mind that often bosses prefer quantitative accomplishments (1% error rate, the lowest in the group) compared to qualitative accomplishments (minimal customer complaints). Make your case on paper first before you go to the boss.

3. Identify whether there is a good time to ask for a raise. Sometimes it's good to ask for a raise as bosses are preparing next year's budget, or around performance reviews. Check with a trusted colleague or mentor to consider timing.

4. Identify the circumstances under which raises are given. If your organization only provides raises only after stellar performance reviews, an off-season raise would be challenging for your boss to approve.

5. You may want to practice this conversation with a friendly partner beforehand. Anticipate what your boss might say and practice how you would respond to various comments. Encourage your partner to keep it as realistic as possible; let them know what you are worried or afraid your boss might say, and practice how you respond.

6. Make sure your reasons for deserving a promotion are professional, not personal. Do not mention that you are buying a new house or that your mother thinks you should be making more. These are not relevant. Focus on the value you provide and what you bring to the organization. Remember, your boss may have to justify the raise to their bosses; give them enough information to do so successfully.

7. Clarify to your boss how you will help the organization grow in the future.

8. If you have data, such as either from your organization or from the field, that shows you are being underpaid relative to your skills and experience, consider discussing a raise as an opportunity to achieve equity with salaries.

9. If your boss says no to a raise, ask for how to improve your performance, or what your boss would like to see before they would approve a raise. You can also ask for an alternative, such as additional paid time off or funding to attend a conference.

10. If your boss says maybe or they will think about it, make sure you clarify next steps. You could say something like, "Thanks for your consideration. Would it be okay for me to check back in with you when we meet again in two weeks?"

11. Be aware that some industries only give raises when you have an offer from another organization and are essentially threatening to leave. If you go this route, be sure you are willing to leave if you don't get the raise. Work with a trusted colleague, mentor, or coach on timing and framing of these conversations.

See also: Challenge 3: Setting goals and priorities

Challenge 13: How to have difficult conversations

Challenge 29: Want feedback on work performance

Challenge 52: Boss gives preferential treatment to others

Take Action: Identify what resources exist for your field that can help you with identifying what appropriate pay ranges are for your position, skills, and experience.

Challenge 36.
You think it's time to move on

You might be ready to start looking for another job. But how do you do that when you're busy at work? How do you know if you should stay or go? How do you determine when you should tell your boss, especially if you need a reference? The good news is that many organizations expect employee turnover to some extent and will not be shocked that an employee is leaving. The bad news is that our bosses are all still just people, who sometimes feel hurt or angry that you're leaving. Here are some ways to navigate this process.

1. Be very clear on the reasons you are considering leaving. Most people leave organizations because they're frustrated with bureaucracy, they aren't receiving feedback, they have a terrible boss, or they no longer have passion for the work. Why do you want to leave?

2. Consider whether it makes sense to leave the organization or to leave for a different part of the organization. Generally, leaving an institution makes sense if many or key relationships in the organization are strained or unsupportive; if you're generally dissatisfied with the institution itself or its leaders' major decisions; or if you want a new challenge or new area to live.

3. Update your LinkedIn and your resume. Ask for feedback from a trusted colleague outside of your organization and ask them how else you can make your information sparkle.

4. Interviewing while employed can be challenging. Usually it's most appropriate to take vacation time/paid time off for interviews. Consider taking a whole day if your interview

clothes are substantially different from your work clothes so you do not have to face questions.

5.   Before you decide to take action on leaving, reassess your goals and priorities. Is there a way your goals can be met in this position? Get very clear on what you want and what the best way is to get it.

6.   A good time to tell your boss you're looking for another job is either when you start to interview (if it's a small field and you think word will get back) or when you are accepting a position (if your boss likely doesn't know and you think they could try to derail the offer), depending on your relationship with your boss.

7.   Before you start to leave, identify a story you can share with prospective employers about why you're leaving. This story should be positive and authentic. You will likely be asked in an interview about why you want to leave your current employer; never say anything bad about them, as the interviewer will assume you will also badmouth your new employer too. Even if you are leaving because your boss is a jerk, ideally you can frame your story about opportunity for growth or contribution at the new organization.

8.   Start identifying projects you may need to wrap up at your current organization and any logistical concerns, such as when your retirement contributions are vested or when insurance may end.

9.   Don't burn bridges as you leave a job. You never know how you may work with this organization or boss or colleagues again. I suggest you start by saying something positive about the job, explain why you're leaving, then help the boss make the transition as easy as possible (such as by being flexible on your last day or describing a transition plan).

10. After you've left, keep in touch with bosses and colleagues with whom you are on good terms. Send a note to let them know you appreciate their kindness, support, or mentoring, and that you hope to say in touch.

See also: Challenge 2: Building your network

Challenge 13: How to have difficult conversations

Challenge 34: Asking for a letter of recommendation

Take Action: Take a long view of your career. Identify what you'd like to be doing/have accomplished 25 years from now. Write it down, and then identify how this position or another one can best support you in achieving those long term accomplishments.

Challenge 37.
Accused of wrongdoing

Sometimes things get serious. Human Resources staff may have obligations to share your conversations with others in the organization. It's good to focus on asking questions. Ideally, you didn't do anything wrong and the situation can be cleared up quickly. In the meantime, it's important to keep a cool head and move forward cautiously.

1. Consider whether you need to consult an attorney. An attorney should be there for you, not for the organization. Don't use the organization's legal benefits if the attorneys are not independent.

2. Consider whether you need to get Human Resources involved. Remember, Human Resources are not primarily employee advocates, but they can assist you in some situations.

3. If there are legal issues, do not confide in colleagues at work, as they could become witnesses for any investigation.

4. Do not delete or copy files or do anything that might look suspicious. Attempts to impede an investigation will have even worse consequences.

5. Generally all information on the organization's devices including computers and cell phones is discoverable in the event of a lawsuit. That means your work phone or work computer's chat history and emails can be taken by lawyers and every document/email/chat history reviewed. Although this is unlikely, don't mix your personal and work devices if you mind your personal devices being potentially reviewed by lawyers. And always communicate in writing at work in ways that you won't be embarrassed of later.

6. Ensure you have support from outside the organization, such as from friends or family.

7. Understand that your colleagues may need to place some distance between them and you while a situation is under investigation. Don't take it personally.

8. Pull together copies of documents that demonstrate your innocence. If you work with an attorney, they will need these.

9. If your character is in question, consider identifying someone senior at the organization and ask if that person could speak on your behalf if needed. Be aware that they might not be able to, and that it's not personal.

10. Take care of yourself physically and emotionally during this time, such as by getting plenty of sleep, eating well, and doing activities you enjoy. Don't let this situation affect your entire existence.

11. Consider whether a leave of absence would be beneficial. Similarly, consider whether changing units would be helpful.

See also: **Challenge 1: Understanding your values**

Challenge 9: Understanding hierarchy at work and when to go around it

Challenge 13: How to have difficult conversations

Take Action: Need help or support? Send me an email jennifer@ leadwithwisdom.com

Part III. Colleague challenges

Challenge 38.
You feel like you are not heard

Sometimes it can feel like we're shouting into the abyss. We may have lots of good ideas but feel like when we speak up, we're ignored or just not acknowledged. Being heard is different from having visibility, as being heard is a much more basic feeling of being acknowledged as part of a team, whereas visibility is related more to positive attention and prominence.

1. Identify what "being heard" would feel like for you. What would it take to feel like you are heard? Consider how to reach those specific goals.

2. Observe how others speak up or don't in different situations and see what you can learn from them.

3. Identify a colleague who is good at speaking up, and ask them how they do it.

4. Be aware that even when people do speak up, some groups are more likely to be heard than others. For example, people may be more likely to listen to people who are white and male than to people with other characteristics. You may want to connect with others who are similar to you to identify how they increase their likelihood of getting heard.

5. Consider what others at your level of seniority are experiencing around speaking up; in some organizations junior people don't get much air time compared to senior people. There may also be some circumstances where you are more likely to be heard (team meeting) than others (organization's annual meeting).

6. Ask your boss privately about the culture at your organization or in your team about speaking up and how they suggest you share ideas most effectively.

7. Let a colleague know you are practicing speaking up and ask for feedback as they observe you.

8. Practice speaking up in environments where you feel most comfortable (or least uncomfortable). Consider letting a colleague know that you are practicing speaking up and ask for their support.

9. If there is a specific meeting where you don't feel heard or specific people who don't seem to hear you, consider whether those meetings or people are good targets for speaking up; it may be they're not worth it.

10. If you have unique characteristics that you think might limit how much you are heard, consider working with a voice coach.

11. Toastmasters is an international organization that helps people improve their public speaking in a safe and friendly environment, including helping people become more comfortable speaking up. Find a Toastmasters group in your area and start going to meetings.

See also: Challenge 5: How to obtain a mentor
             Challenge 24: Shy/introverted
             Challenge 27: Hard to make small talk
             Challenge 30: Want more visibility

Take Action: When is the last time you felt you were not heard at work? What could you change about the situation knowing what you know now?

Challenge 39.
Colleagues frequently interrupt you

You're having a conversation and then – wham! – a colleague cuts you off. Although this happens sometimes, when it becomes a pattern, it needs to be addressed.

1. Talk with the person who interrupts you to request that they stop interrupting you. For example, you can say, "I notice you often cut me off when I'm not done talking. I would appreciate it if you wouldn't do that." Stand your ground.

2. Observe other colleagues who may be shy or soft-spoken and identify how they manage interruptions.

3. Ask a trusted colleague for advice on how to manage interruptions.

4. Take notes in a meeting so that when you speak up you can complete your thought completely and confidently.

5. Observe the environment and identify where people frequently interrupt each other due to excitement or joy or whether they interrupt others as a power play. If it's the former, that is less toxic and you may be able to adjust your expectations.

6. In a meeting where you were interrupted, follow up with the meeting leader or the whole group with an email to explain your point and request it be addressed at the next meeting.

7. If you notice patterns in who is interrupting and who is being interrupted, talk with your boss or a trusted colleague about how to address the situation.

8. Practice responses with a friend for different ways to react when someone interrupts you.

9. If you feel like you are being interrupted due to low confidence, practice activities outside of work that help you increase confidence such as martial arts, triathlons, or rock climbing.

10. Try out a few different ways to stop someone when they attempt to interrupt you. For example, you could say, "That's a good point, but I want to make sure that we emphasize...." Or, "I'd like to finish what I was saying before we move on."

11. Talk to someone you trust outside of work for an outside opinion on whether any of your conversational styles may inadvertently encourage interruptions. For example, people who are very longwinded or who talk slowly tend to be interrupted more frequently. Being aware of these styles doesn't mean you have to change them, but it would help you adjust your expectations.

12. It is important to manage your feelings about being interrupted until your efforts to address it are heard. For example, yelling or displaying anger at interruptions may end with you looking worse than the interrupter.

13. If you find you are being repeatedly interrupted across multiple situations, you may want to consider obtaining a coach who can help you identify how best to deal with this challenge.

See also: Challenge 28: Difficulty speaking in public/giving presentations

Challenge 38: You feel like you are not heard

Challenge 49: Colleagues are aggressive, racist, sexist, homophobic or hostile

Challenge 54: Boss bullies you

Take Action: When you're interrupted next, how will you respond? What are your top 3 go-to steps that feel like the best steps to take before reacting too quickly?

Challenge 40.
Meetings are frustrating

Meeting can be challenging, both as someone running the meeting and as someone attending. It is possible to have useful meetings! It depends on how they're used and how everyone approaches them. Even if you are not running the meeting, you can contribute to running better meetings.

1. Ask for the agenda for each meeting if your position allows.

2. If you are running the meeting, use the first few minutes of each meeting to clarify the intent of the meeting, ensure the right people are at the table to make decisions, and get updates on the task items from the last meeting. If you are not running the meeting, see if you can speak up and ask about these things yourself.

3. If you are running the meeting, clarify that you expect people to participate in the meeting. If they are too junior or too uncomfortable to actively participate, talk with them individually to identify any problems and help them feel more comfortable speaking up.

4. If many people are uncomfortable speaking up, go around the table and ask each person to provide one suggestion, their opinion, etc., to move the conversation. If you are not leading the meeting, feel free to ask others what they think, such as by saying, "Mary, I'm wondering what you're thinking about this."

5. Help keep people on topic and on track by gently redirecting to the topics on the agenda and tabling other topics for the end if there's time or for the next meeting. It may be helpful

to use a whiteboard or large notepad to list topics to come back to.

6. Clearly document all decisions made in the meeting including which person will be responsible to do what and by when. Clarify expectations that people will give updates on items in their purview at each meeting and that you expect there to be progress between each meeting.

7. Make a list of what meetings you attend. Then consider the value of each regarding how much they are helpful to achieve goals and priorities. Consider discussing with your staff or your boss to identify which meetings need to be improved and which you should no longer attend.

8. In the last few minutes of the meeting, make note of the time ("I notice we have about 10 minutes left in the meeting…"), and review what has been accomplished and what next steps have been identified. Ensure these are written in the notes.

9. If you are running the meeting, consider asking a junior person to take over running a meeting. First talk with them about it and have them observe you run the meeting, then have them take over running the meeting while you observe them, then have them run the meeting during your absence with them reporting back to you what successes and challenges they experienced.

10. If there is a person in the meeting who is disruptive or who frequently gets the meeting off track, talk with that person individually to request that they help the meetings move forward positively.

11. If there is a person who does not seem empowered by their boss to make decisions or contribute in the meeting, talk to the person about how to improve the situation.

12. Mix up the less exciting tasks such as note-taking or writing meeting minutes so it's not always the same person who has to do this kind of work.

See also: Challenge 4: When and how to obtain a mentor

Challenge 10: Building relationships with colleagues

Challenge 21: Want to improve time management/ organization

Challenge 31: Want to increase influence

Take Action: What's your favorite tip from the above that you can begin using at your next meeting?

Challenge 41.
Annoying office mate

If your office mate smells, brings stinky food, wears too much perfume, chews loudly, is on too many personal calls, or is otherwise annoying, don't give up hope! There are many ways to address these "stinky" problems!

1. Consider whether the annoyance may be something the person cannot control, such as related to a physical or emotional condition. Have empathy just in case.

2. Ask your colleague about the annoyance, by saying, for example, "Did you realize you make a clicking noise? It's very distracting." It's possible the person doesn't know what they're doing (making noises) or doesn't realize it's annoying. Most people will generally apologize and agree to stop the annoying thing. If not, state clearly that you request they stop or do the activity elsewhere.

3. Adjust your expectations that someone will completely stop being annoying. Try to ignore the annoying behavior, laugh at it, or pretend it doesn't exist.

4. If you have a situation that is potentially medically concerning, such as a food allergy or perfume sensitivity, consider involving your boss or Human Resources for assistance if the person is not immediately forthcoming.

5. Consider if there is anything you can do on your end, such as wearing headphones to buffer noise.

6. Consider bringing up the issue to a boss privately so he or she can identify how to help you move forward. Be careful to keep

the conversation focused on you (for example, "I am allergic to..." or "I find it hard to focus when...") so the conversation doesn't become an attack on one person.

7. You may change your behavior in a way to make the situation more palatable; for example, if they always bring fish for lunch on Fridays, and that is hard for you to be around, you could arrange to go out for lunch or work from home that day.

8. Be mindful of maintaining your integrity and to the greatest extent possible, protecting the other person's dignity in handling this issue. Even though you might feel angry or disgusted or frustrated, keep it professional and don't gossip to coworkers about it.

9. Talk with your boss to see if there are ways to be flexible. For example, if you are very sensitive to smells, you may ask if you could switch desks with someone so you are not sitting next to the break room.

10. If there are general office rules that work in your favor, such as a rule against playing music without headphones, you may be able to reference those rules when you discuss with your colleague.

See also: Challenge 10: Building relationships with colleagues
Challenge 13: How to have difficult conversations
Challenge 19: Easily distracted

Action Step: Imagine you're the person on the receiving end; how would you like to be approached about the issue? Put yourself in their shoes. Write out how you'd like to see the conversation going.

Challenge 42.
Colleague doesn't contribute

From grade school projects to day-to-day work, sometimes our colleagues just don't pull their own weight. No need to get angry – just try some strategies to help things move forward.

1. Start by assuming the person has something else getting in the way of completing their work as opposed to they are just refusing to work. Check with them and see if there is something else going on.

2. Ask the colleague if they are having trouble completing their part of the work and why. There might be a way to assist them, suggest resources, or otherwise address the impasse.

3. Clarify with the colleague who is responsible for what and make notes. If there are differences of opinion, try to work it out with your colleague.

4. If your colleague still doesn't do their part, follow up with a written email saying, "As we discussed, you said you could finish [x] by today and it hasn't been completed. I haven't had the opportunity to review it. Could please send it to me so I can review?" If possible, tie the request to a key result or deliverable that is dependent on their task being delivered: "It's important we finish this project on time so we can proceed to the next step." Be extra careful about tone in emails and ask someone to read it over before you send it to be safe.

5. Go to your boss for assistance in sorting out the situation.

6. Consider forwarding resources to assist with a project, or suggesting someone to contact if they are having difficulty.

7. If appropriate (such as if you are getting stonewalled), ask a status question in a more public setting so that your roles can be agreed upon in public. You can say, "John was working on this part of the project. John, could you give us an update on the status of the project?"

8. Set clear boundaries and be sure not to take on the other person's work responsibilities. Being professional and thoughtful doesn't mean you do their work. Find that balance.

9. Move your conversations from less formal to more formal by having a meeting with the colleague, providing an agenda, and sharing notes on what was agreed. If appropriate, copy your boss on the emails.

10. If this is a pattern with this particular colleague not doing their work, ask to be reassigned to a project not working with this colleague.

11. You may want to consider obtaining a coach who can help you through this challenge.

See also: Challenge 1: Understanding your values

Challenge 10: Building relationships with colleagues

Challenge 18: Feel negative about work

Challenge 43: Colleagues take credit for your work

Take Action: Given the situation you're currently in, what feels like the best win-win situation for both you and your colleague? Free write below and come up with your unique action plan.

Challenge 43.
Colleagues take credit for your work

You worked with a colleague on a project, but they present it as their own and don't acknowledge your contributions. It is so frustrating when someone else takes credit for your work! There are several ways to address this issue so it doesn't happen more than once.

1. For a new project, attempt to clarify who will do what parts of the projects, and how credit will be allocated.

2. Try to work with colleagues who share responsibility and credit if possible.

3. Talk to the person who took credit for your work to let them know you saw what they did and that it wasn't cool.

4. Build relationships with colleagues; they may be less likely to take credit for your work if they have a genuine connection with you.

5. Keep notes about who is doing what for each project. This documentation may come in handy later to refresh your memory if you need it.

6. Limit how you share information you may find sensitive if you think they might not use it well or might use it against you.

7. Consider talking to your boss or the person running the project to clarify what happened and ask for advice regarding how to proceed.

8. Observe the environment where you work to identify if this is a common and accepted occurrence or whether it is generally

discouraged. If it is a common and accepted occurrence, consider whether this is the right work environment for you.

9. Identify which types of projects can be done alone versus which need to be split amongst employees. Think about which person has the proper expertise for the subject area, so roles and contribution can be defined early.

10. Consider meeting with colleagues to discuss how credit is allocated. Can you all share credit, or take turns having primary credit across different projects so you all benefit? You can also develop this meeting into an informal peer mentoring group.

11. If it happens frequently that you feel like people are taking advantage of you, you may want to consider obtaining a therapist who can help you through this challenge so that you can break the patterns and feel better.

See also: Challenge 1: Understanding your values

Challenge 10: Building relationships with colleagues

Challenge 18: Feel negative about work

Challenge 42: Colleague doesn't contribute

Take Action: Write out your revenge – every last detail – and reflect: Is this how you want to be seen or heard? (Probably not.) Instead of revenge, what's the best way for you to express this issue? Get clear before taking action.

Challenge 44.
Colleagues are extremely competitive

Organizations and fields vary in the degree of competition between employees. High levels of competition can feel very uncomfortable if you're not used to it.

1. Observe the environment where you work to identify if this is a common and accepted occurrence or whether it is generally discouraged. If it is a common and accepted occurrence, consider whether this is the right work environment for you. Consider if being more competitive is consistent with your values or your approach to work. If not, this may not be the job, field, or organization for you.

2. You may want to increase your competitiveness. Consider what is in line with your values and how to improve your skills at competing.

3. Identify how merit raises, promotions, and praise are provided and delivered. For example, some units or organizations manage merit raises as a zero sum game (where one wins and the other loses), whereas other groups provide merit raises equally to all members of the team based on collective team performance. Consider if the way your field, organization, or unit manages these limited resources is in line with your values.

4. Consider whether what you are observing is healthy tension, in which two teams simply have opposing goals (e.g., one team needs to get it submitted fast and another team is responsible for checking all details for accuracy). Healthy tension should still be respectful. Bring both teams together to voice their concerns so that both groups can be more successful together.

5. Identify a colleague who is competitive and ask them about their approach to work relationships.

6. Talk to someone you trust outside of work for an outside opinion.

7. Consider gender, race, ethnicity, sexual orientation, and disability status regarding how you're perceiving the situation or how you are being perceived.

8. Consider the value in being a neutral player. That could mean you are less likely to be promoted, or it could mean you become trusted by everyone. Identify if neutrality is a workable stance for you.

9. Consider taking part in extracurricular sports activities with your organization, such as on the softball team. It may give you a different perspective of how competition works in the organization.

10. You may want to consider obtaining a coach who can help you through how you can best respond to your colleagues' competitiveness.

See also: Challenge 1: Understanding your values
Challenge 10: Building relationships with colleagues
Challenge 13: How to have difficult conversations
Challenge 38: You feel like you are not heard

Take Action: What makes you feel the most confident? It could be anything! Write it all out below. Notice anything that's calling you in to connect even more to your confidence level?

Challenge 45.
Backstabbing

Some people are just jerks. Others are generally nice people who sometimes do jerky things. A colleague told me how hurt he was when someone told him that they were supporting his promotion yet wrote a very negative letter recommending against promotion to the committee. Ouch! Backstabbing, which is when someone criticizes or undermines you while feigning friendship, can be painful. It's best not to let it happen more than once.

1. Limit the information you share with colleagues to reduce the amount of ammunition they have on you. Be extremely judicious with sharing any personal information, including about problems you are struggling with or any personal issues.

2. Consider what the backstabber's motive might be – is it personal to them, just business, competition, or is this just their way of acting? Understanding their motives may help you understand how to counter them and protect yourself.

3. Consider whether it would make sense to confront the backstabber. If you do, stick to the facts and identify what you observed and ask for their perspective, such as by saying, "It seemed like this was intentional; can you help me understand what happened?" If they don't respond kindly and by attempting to make the situation better, stay away.

4. Consider whether it is possible to avoid the backstabber if possible and if doing so would not harm you professionally.

5. Talk to someone you trust outside of work for an outside opinion.

6. Pull together copies of documents that demonstrate your role in this situation – have "receipts" you can go back to.

7. Consider meeting with colleagues to compare experiences. You can also develop this meeting into an informal mentoring group.

8. If it is possible and if the backstabbing is isolated to one or two people, consider switching groups or teams in your organization so you are not working with the backstabber.

9. Consider talking with your boss about the organization's perspective on civility and courtesy generally to understand their perspective and see if they may be an ally. Speak tactfully and be cautious not to fuel workplace drama with your boss.

10. Consider whether it may make sense to limit your public expressions of disappointment or hurt. Sometimes it is better to not give backstabbers the satisfaction.

11. Observe the environment where you work to identify if this is a common and accepted occurrence or whether it is generally discouraged. If it is a common and accepted occurrence, consider whether this is the right work environment for you.

See also: **Challenge 10: Building relationships with colleagues**

               Challenge 18: Feel negative about work

               Challenge 54: Boss bullies you

               Challenge 63: Boss undermines you

Take Action: Exercise allows you to release frustration and create a clear mind. What's your favorite form of movement? Go do that, then come back and write down your approach and dealing with that backstabber. Notice how your energy changed?

Challenge 46.
Colleagues over-disclose personal information

Sometimes you learn things about your colleagues you just didn't want to know. They keep sharing information about their family, their medical problems, or their lives that are not work-appropriate or just way too much.

1. Do not reciprocate by sharing personal information when a colleague over-discloses. Instead, provide neutral responses ("Oh, that sounds difficult") or responses that end the conversation ("I'm sorry, I have to go to a meeting.").

2. Observe what kind of information about personal lives is generally disclosed and how it happens. For example, do bosses typically ask how their staff will use their vacation days or what illness they were experiencing when they call out sick? Both of those are indicators that this environment may tolerate over-disclosure (or at least that this boss does). Your comfort with high disclosure may vary; high disclosure could become a problem if you have private health or personal information you'd rather not be shared, or if personal information is used in work decisions (e.g., "We understand you're coming back from leave after your mother's passing, so we gave a high-profile project to someone else"). Identify if this is organization-wide or limited to this group only.

3. Have a selection of vague answers ready that provide minimal information if you are asked these questions. For example, if you are asked about what you did on vacation, you can say you stayed at home or traveled with friends if you don't want to discuss your personal living situation.

4. If people respond to your minimal information with judgmental comments (for example, if you tell them you went to the beach on vacation and they say, "Oh, that sounds expensive!" or "How did you afford that?") end the conversation and share even less next time.

5. Do not share personal information in areas where you are not sure you are alone (e.g., in a bathroom).

6. Talk to someone you trust outside of work for an outside opinion of what is appropriate sharing at their workplace.

7. You may want to have a variety of responses that help redirect the colleague back to work conversations, such as, "Okay. Now about this report..." or "Huh. As I was saying..."

8. Be aware of and possibly limit the amount of personal information you share passively, such as photos and mementos on your desk. This can help set the expectation that you are there to work.

9. Unfriend or unfollow a colleague on social media if you feel you're being exposed to too much personal information.

10. If someone is describing significant problems with their family or medical issues that are interfering with their work or causing them distress, you may want to recommend they speak to their boss or Human Resources about resources or taking leave so they can address these issues. Constant complaints could mean they are not pulling their own weight at work, or it could mean they have lots of challenges in their life right now; either way, let Human Resources sort it out. It's not your place to. Assume good intentions.

11. Resist the urge to offer advice or to weigh in on their stories. Responding neutrally then leaving or changing the subject is best.

See also: Challenge 13: How to have difficult conversations

Challenge 19: Easily Distracted

Challenge 22: Difficulty saying no

Take Action: Do a little research to identify the contact person in the Human Resources office so you can reference if you ever need.

Challenge 47.
Gossipy colleagues

Gossip is not always bad. Every organization relies on word of mouth to pass information and opportunities along. Good strategic information is invaluable for helping you climb the ladder. Every organization, however, also has a few gossips who seem to revel in negative information about people. These are the people who delight in passing along negative information about other people or stirring up problems. It's important to know the difference between word of mouth information and negative gossip and to not engage with mean-spirited gossips.

1. Do not engage in negative gossip about people, either to listen or to pass along.

2. When people start to gossip, walk away or find something else to do.

3. It may be that when you are not present, you will be gossiped about. Keep the amount of information you share to a minimum to reduce what they can share about you.

4. Don't feel like you have to spend time with gossips in order not to be the target of negative gossip.

5. Create a mantra you can use when people try to pull you into negative gossip, such as, "Huh. I don't see it that way" or "I don't feel comfortable talking about Brenda like that when she's not here."

6. Identify someone who seems very good at staying out of negative gossip and ask them how they do it.

7. Read the book *No More Team Drama: Ending the Gossip, Cliques, and Other Crap that Damage Workplace Teams* by Joe Mull to get more insight on how to reduce gossip and build relationships (details listed in the "For further reading" section).

8. Consider that some people often do know about useful information before others. Consider carefully if you choose to engage to trade information with them. Be sure you are acting in accordance with your values and sense of integrity and not engaging in anything negative or that you will regret.

9. Do not share private information or negative gossip in areas where you are not sure you are alone (e.g., in a bathroom).

10. Limit your social media relationship with colleagues who typically engage in negative gossip. You may want to maximize your social media relationships with people who share useful positive or neutral information.

11. If you're having a problem at work, talk to someone you trust outside of work for an external opinion. Don't vent to work colleagues as it might end up in gossip.

12. If you feel you must engage with some office gossip, provide very general and non-controversial information and then leave the conversation.

13. If you frequently find yourself on the receiving end of negative gossip, you may want to consider obtaining help from a coach or therapist who can help you strategize how to change these patterns.

See also: Challenge 10: Building relationships with colleagues

Challenge 16: Feel isolated

Challenge 22: Difficulty saying no

Challenge 25: Overly concerned or underconcerned about others' feelings

Take action: Pledge to not contribute to gossip and to share only positive, supportive information about your colleagues.

Challenge 48.
Colleague pesters you for a date or harasses you

It can to anyone across all spectrums of gender and sexuality: a colleague doesn't know that no means no, or continues to make sexual comments around you or even touches you without your permission. This is one of the most frightening and upsetting experiences people have at work. Many of us struggle with wanting the perpetrator to stop and the very real possibility that speaking up can hurt <u>your</u> career. Here are some ways to address this stressful situation.

1. If someone asks you out and you don't want to go out with them, be explicit and clear in your "no." If you leave room for doubt, the person may misunderstand and ask again.

2. If you happen to know a friend who experienced sexual harassment, you may want to let them know what is happening to you and ask what they recommend.

3. Know your rights: In the U.S., repeated unwanted sexual comments, propositions, or touching can be considered sexual harassment and can be against the law. Some behavior is egregious if committed only once. Know what is and is not acceptable behavior legally. The U.S. Equal Employment Opportunity Commission has definitions.

4. Check your organization's policies for how they address sexual harassment. This policy will outline acceptable and unacceptable behavior and indicate whom to contact if there is a problem.

5. Observe the culture of your organization to identify how much sexualized talk (including jokes and memes) is commonplace and accepted. The more it is accepted, the more difficult it

might be for you to succeed in getting the perpetrator to stop. If this is the case, consider changing organizations.

6. If you are in the U.S. or employed by a U.S.-based company, you have the right to contact the Equal Employment Opportunity Commission if you feel you are being discriminated against because of your gender, including repeated, unwanted sexual comments or propositions.

7. Be very clear with messages you are sending to individuals regarding your personal life. If there is ever a misunderstanding about your intentions or your boundaries, state explicitly that you want their behavior to stop. If it continues, escalate to someone else at your organization.

8. If it's possible to avoid the person, keep some distance.

9. Strength in numbers: spend time with people in a similar group as you, such as age, professional level, etc., so you're not alone with this person.

10. Consider whether it might make sense to transfer units within the organization if other methods don't work to get the person to stop.

11. Consider national organizations and support groups that can provide information and resources, such as #metoo; the Rape, Abuse & Incest National Network (rainn.org), leanin.org, and others.

See also: Challenge 9: Understanding hierarchy at work and when to go around it

Challenge 13: How to have difficult conversations with people

Challenge 25: Overly concerned or underconcerned about others' feelings

Challenge 49: Colleagues are aggressive, racist, sexist, homophobic, or hostile

Take Action: Remember that Human Resources number from #46? Now is the time to follow up if needed.

Challenge 49.
Colleagues are aggressive, racist, sexist, homophobic, or hostile

I hope you never have to deal with aggressive, racist, sexist, homophobic, or hostile colleagues. If you do, I want you to have tools to deal with the situation in the moment and to take it to the appropriate higher-ups at your organization so it stops.

1. It shouldn't feel necessary but state clearly what you are requesting. For example, "Please don't use that word around me. It makes me uncomfortable."

2. If the person claims they are kidding around, you can say, "I don't appreciate jokes about [x]. Please stop."

3. If it's possible to confront someone privately, you are more likely to have a productive conversation with the person. If there are others around who are being affected by the comment or action, you may want to consider standing up in front of others intentionally, especially if you know they will have your back.

4. Consider the difference between a request and a demand. You can start with a request ("please don't use that word") and then escalate to a demand if needed. For example, "We all enjoy joking around, but jokes about racial groups are not funny, and I won't listen anymore." Then walk away.

5. Document what happened including the date, location, people present, and what happened, even if in your own file. Have "receipts" you can go back to.

6. Get support from others, including friends or family. Be cautious discussing the situation too broadly within the

organization, especially if it could possibly lead to legal action for discrimination.

7. The great Catherine Morrison provided an example of how to respond to an underhanded comment, simply by connecting an observation with a statement of its impact: "I see you smiling, but that feels like a dig."

8. If coworkers are being loud and obnoxious, you can attempt to reign in the conversation. For example, "Let's get back to the agenda. Next was…"

9. It's important to speak up when you hear inappropriate comments. If you don't speak up, it often gives the impression that you are condoning them even if you are not.

10. Consider contacting your boss, Human Resources (which is there to protect the organization), or a lawyer (who is there to protect you) if discriminatory language or actions do not stop. If you need to find a lawyer, contact a local university law school for an inexpensive or low cost referral or Google "best employment lawyer" with the name of your town and call to ask for a free consultation

See also: Challenge 9: Understanding hierarchy at work and when to go around it

Challenge 22: Difficulty saying no

Challenge 36: You think it's time to move on

Challenge 60: Don't feel supported by boss

Take Action: Get support from a close friend or colleague so you can decide what to do.

Part IV. Boss challenges

Challenge 50.
Boss doesn't lead

If you have a hands-off, distant boss who doesn't support you or just wants to be liked, you can have a hard time getting your work done. Though you're not responsible for fixing your boss, you may find some ways to help work around their lack of leadership.

1. Be aware that not all bosses are successful leaders. Identify what you are able to learn from this job and this boss.

2. Identify what your boss does well.

3. Be careful to not usurp your boss's authority, even if they are not using it well.

4. Do not confront your boss on what you perceive to be their lack of leadership. That is not likely to go well. Know that if you are seeing your boss's challenges, other people probably see it as well, even if they can't say anything to you. You are not alone.

5. Identify job duties that do not rely on your boss and focus on those.

6. Review your short-term or long-term plan and identify how your boss may be able to teach you or help you despite not leading much.

7. Observe how other people work with this boss and how they interact with them.

8. Consider providing suggestions. "I found a few possible solutions to this problem. What do you think?"

9. Talk to someone you trust outside of your team for perspective on how to work with your boss. Be very diplomatic and stay away from gossip. You don't want your complaints to get back to your boss in a negative way. It often helps to ask someone for advice about the challenge, rather than starting with a complaint. Make sure to have alternate explanations. For example, "I'm wondering if you could help me with a problem. I am working on a project and not getting much guidance from my boss. I know they're really busy, but I'm not sure how to address this. What do you suggest?"

10. Identify someone who works well with your boss (or at least who works successfully with them!) and ask them for suggestions.

11. Remember you are responsible only for yourself and your work. You may try to protect your boss or your team, but you are not responsible for your boss's approach to work. Be careful how you invest your energy.

12. Identify what is bothering you about your boss not leading. If it's just a principle issue (such as, they are getting paid to lead!) you may want to consider letting the principle go for a while and address the day-to-day challenges that affect you.

13. Make sure to get an answer from your boss before you leave the room. Finish the conversations by asking, "I'll get started with this, okay?" or "I want to confirm you're okay to move it forward."

14. Consider where the lack of leadership affects you the most (meetings, professional development, etc.) and address each topic separately with your boss.

15. You may want to consider obtaining a coach who can help you through this challenge.

See also: Challenge 3: Setting goals and priorities

Challenge 4: When and how to obtain a mentor

Challenge 36: You think it's time to move on

Challenge 60: Don't feel supported by boss

Take Action: Need support to listen to what's happening in your work and world? Email me at Jennifer@leadwithwisdom.com.

Challenge 51.
Boss takes credit for your work

Many of us have had the experience of a colleague who is a lurker on a project...until it's time to take credit for what's been accomplished. When your boss takes credit for your work, there are ways to address this.

1. Understand that many times bosses are expected to take credit for work presented, and it may be unusual in your organization or field to list names of everyone who contributed to a project. Still, it would be nice if they did!

2. If the project has clear credit responsibility, such as a published article, report, or book, discuss *in advance* with your boss how credit will be allocated.

3. If you are looking to advance in the field and would like to increase your visibility, talk with your boss about opportunities to increase your visibility on projects to which you contributed.

4. Consider how asking for credit may affect your long-term career goals.

5. Ask your boss for guidelines for how work is credited, and offer to take more responsibility to receive named credit if that is an option.

6. Talk to someone you trust outside of your company but in your field for an external opinion of how credit is managed for staff at your level. If staff at your level is typically credited by name, you may want to consider how to best move up or discuss credit on additional projects.

7. Be aware that it could be considered rude in your field to ask for named credit on a project. Observe what the standards are before making waves.

8. Regardless of official named credit, you should keep track of your contributions to each project so that you can discuss them as needed. These notes can also be helpful for you to discuss at performance review time, to add to your resume and as possible talking points for future interviews.

9. Consider consulting your field's ethical guidelines regarding named contributions. For example, in medicine, all individuals who contributed substantially to a scientific manuscript are expected to be credited as authors. Others may be credited in the acknowledgements. If your organization follows these guidelines, discuss them with your boss at the beginning of projects so you are on the same page. For example, "substantial contribution" can be interpreted quite differently by different people.

10. Identify someone senior to you who works well with your boss and ask them how they manage assessing credit.

11. Identify people who previously worked with your boss and ask them for tips in how to manage assessment of credit.

See also: Challenge 1: Understanding your values
Challenge 3: Setting goals and priorities
Challenge 38: You feel like you are not heard

Take Action: From the above tips, what action step makes the most sense given your situation?

Challenge 52.
Boss gives preferential treatment to others

It can come to you like a punch in the gut: you find out a colleague doing the same work has been getting paid more than you or getting plum assignments that you weren't even invited to consider. Sometimes a person more junior to you is hired at a higher rate – to be your boss! These situations shouldn't happen, and yet they do. While you're steaming about the unfairness, here are some practical suggestions.

1. Take a big breath and don't say anything you'll regret later. Even though it seems unfair, you don't have all the facts. Better to figure out what is happening first and provide a reasoned response. Losing your cool only makes you look bad.

2. See if there are patterns you can identify. Are the people getting preferential treatment older, the boss's friends, something else? Try to sleuth out a counterfactual: What else could possibly explain this situation?

3. Consider talking with your boss about the perceived inequality. Keep the focus on the perception, and ask politely for an explanation. For example, you could say, "I noticed the last three business trips went to Pat. Can you help me understand how you make decisions on who gets to go on trips? I'm interested in traveling as well."

4. If you really want to push the issue more, you can ask the question in a group meeting. This strategy has risks, can irritate your boss, and may make it less likely you will get what you want. If you decide to address it in a meeting, have pre-conversations with others who will be there and ensure you have allies who will speak up about the issue so you are not alone in your concern.

5. If there is a salary issue or something that may not be in your boss's direct control, consider going to Human Resources to ask the question. Present yourself as curious, not livid. For example, "I happened to find out that there are some significant discrepancies in salary among us coders. Could you help me understand how salaries are determined, and why they are so different when we are doing the same job?" Do not let the other person take the conversation into how you found this information. If they ask about that, say, "Could you confirm whether the discrepancies I'm presenting to you are real? That's more important than how the information came to me." Ideally, they will offer to review salaries and conduct an equity adjustment.

6. You may want to contact a lawyer if you are not getting information from Human Resources or your boss. Remember, Human Resources staff may not always be able to advocate for you, but they can assist you in many situations, especially if your interests align with those of the organization. A lawyer can help you understand your options and let you know the likelihood that you will receive an outcome you desire. If you need to find a lawyer, contact a local university law school for an inexpensive or low cost referral or Google "best employment lawyer" with the name of your town and call to ask for a free consultation.

7. Some industries have salary information available. Contact your trade organization (anonymously if you want) to ask about where to find average salaries for your field.

8. This is a great topic to discuss with a mentor or trusted colleague. Present your observations and ask how they would proceed. Keep in mind you can win the battle and lose the war – consider the longer-term consequences and whether those are worth it.

9. Sometimes things just aren't fair. It's wrong and awful and you can't fix it. If this is one of those situations, try to find a way to cope – whether it's leaving the job, moving to another work team, or continuing to work toward equity.

10. As you advance at work and have more power or employees, remember the importance of equity and ensure you are being fair to others. Stand up for staff who are climbing the ladder after you.

See also: Challenge 2: Building your network

Challenge 3: Setting goals and priorities

Challenge 4: When and how to obtain a mentor

Challenge 9: Understanding hierarchy at work and when to go around it

Take Action: If you feel something is unfair, examine the evidence, ask questions, and decide how to proceed. Do something about it or let it go if at all possible.

Challenge 53.
Boss does not mentor you

A mentor is someone who is committed to your growth and professional development. Typically, mentors help you learn what you need to know on the job and how to improve. Sometimes, however, bosses aren't required to mentor, don't like to mentor, aren't aware you need mentoring, or may even be unsupportive of your professional development. Other times, mentorship "just happens" organically. If you have a boss who wants to mentor, that is great, but that is a bonus, not to be expected.

1. Remember you are responsible for your own professional development and career growth. When bosses help us, that is wonderful, but ultimately, it's up to us.

2. Adjust your expectations to identify ways in which your boss may be supportive of you even if they do not provide the mentorship you would like. It is not reasonable to expect one person to provide all of your mentoring needs.

3. Read professional publications in your field so you can learn about current issues and important developments.

4. Conduct a self-assessment to understand areas you feel you need mentoring. Identify if you need skills development, more knowledge, support, or just more practice or confidence.

5. Be alert for opportunities to learn from your colleagues.

6. Identify a colleague who is skilled in an area you want to learn and ask them how they do it. You can also ask for advice on how to improve your skills in that area.

7. Go to professional conferences or presentations in your field, so you can keep up with current issues and important developments (and possibly find a mentor!).

8. Identify professional development programs in your company or professional association so you can learn what is needed to be successful in your field.

9. Consider reviewing your company's Human Resources website or talking with a Human Resources associate about what professional development opportunities might be available. Sign up for newsletters with different organizations in your field to be aware of opportunities.

10. See the reference section for books about mentoring.

11. Talk with your boss about your strengths and areas for improvement. Discuss ways to identify where you might be able to get this support. For example, let your boss know you're interested in a topic and ask if they know someone who could help you with it.

12. Identify someone other than your boss who can mentor you on these specific topics.

13. Consider meeting with others at your level of experience and seniority and comparing job duties, expectations, needs, etc. You can also develop this meeting into an informal mentoring group. If one doesn't exist, consider starting one.

See also: Challenge 2: Building your network

Challenge 4: When and how to obtain a mentor

Challenge 10: Building relationships with colleagues

Challenge 29: Want feedback on work performance

Take Action: What are your skills? What would you like to learn more about? Take a few steps from the tips above to begin putting them into motion.

Challenge 54.
Boss bullies you

Bullies aren't just for grade school: Some people never grow out of bullying others. You don't have to put up with bullies!

1. Clarify what kind of bullying is happening: Does it directly affect your work? Is it about your work? Is it about your personal life (beliefs, appearance, religion, sexual orientation, race, gender, age, or gender presentation)? This could determine the way you need to deal with it. Generally bullying related to gender, race, and religion could be considered unlawful harassment at work, whereas other kinds of bullying may not be.

2. Read *The Asshole Survival Guide: How to Deal with People who Treat you Like Dirt* by Robert Sutton (details listed in the "For further reading" section).

3. Remember, it is a reflection on your boss, not on you, if you are bullied.

4. Document incidents of bullying, even if it's only in your own note log. Consider emailing notes to yourself so you have a time/date stamp.

5. Consider if you want to respond and stand up for yourself. There are positive and negative aspects for each option.

6. Consider talking with appropriate individuals such as people in your chain of command, Human Resources, or Corporate Compliance, even anonymously, to identify what steps can be taken.

7. Identify someone senior to you who works well with your boss and ask them how they manage when your boss gets upset.

8. Identify colleagues who can stand up for you. Sometimes even when you can't defend yourself, someone else can defend you, and then you can defend each other.

9. Identify people who previously worked with your boss and ask them for tips in how to manage your boss's moods.

10. If your efforts aren't working, consider that this may be an unsustainable situation and you may need to seek employment elsewhere.

11. Talk to someone you trust outside of work for an outside opinion.

12. You may want to consider obtaining a coach who can help you through this challenge.

13. If you have a pattern of being bullied, you may want to consider talking with a therapist about how to break these patterns.

See also: Challenge 9: Understanding hierarchy at work and when to go around it

Challenge 13: How to have difficult conversations

Challenge 45: Backstabbing

Take Action: Looking for a group to express your thoughts and feelings? Join the Lead with Wisdom Community for Millennials at https://www.facebook.com/groups/295731811374991/, to connect with others just like yourself as a safe space to connect and communicate with each other on issues just like this.

Challenge 55.
Boss asks me to do work outside of official duties

Usually job duties are pretty clear, but sometimes bosses reach outside of what's appropriate to ask you to do personal tasks for them. There are very few circumstances in which this is acceptable (such as a job as a personal assistant or possibly if you have a pre-existing relationship), and for most day jobs, these are not okay asks.

1. Review your job description to ensure you are clear on what is and is not your role.

2. Read your organization's policies and standards for professional conduct to ensure you understand the requirements. If there are special circumstances, such as federal funding or financial regulations that apply, make sure you understand the limits of these.

3. Observe what others in your organization do so that you have an understanding of what individuals in your kind of position are expected to do for their bosses or more senior people.

4. If you disagree with tasks your boss asks you to complete, you have options. You can let your boss know you feel it is inappropriate. You can let someone else (e.g., Human Resources or the Ombudsman's Office) know you feel it is inappropriate. You could also consider whether this is the position you want.

5. If the action is illegal or harmful to others, you are well within your rights to not do the action and to raise a whistleblower complaint.

6. Identify someone senior to you who works well with your boss and ask them how they manage when your boss asks them for extra work.

7. Identify people who previously worked with your boss and ask them for tips in how to manage your boss's extra-curricular requests.

8. Ask a trusted colleague about the culture at the company regarding doing favors/work outside of official duties.

9. Talk to someone you trust outside of work for an outside opinion.

10. You may want to consider obtaining a coach who can help you through this challenge.

See also: Challenge 1: Understanding your values

Challenge 4: When and how to obtain a mentor

Challenge 9: Understanding hierarchy at work and when to go around it

Challenge 22: Difficulty saying no

Take Action: If this is happening now, review your job description and take action on the items above. You're not in the wrong if your boundaries are being crossed.

Challenge 56.
Boss insults you in front of others

Ideally, bosses support and praise you in public, and wait for a private meeting to raise criticisms and concerns. Sometimes, however, bosses will say insulting or demeaning things about you in front of others.

1. When the insult happens, observe the others to determine if they are also shocked or surprised. If they are, it will confirm that your feelings and reactions are not misplaced, and these people may become your allies in getting the behavior to stop.

2. Consider what kind of response may be appropriate at the time, including perhaps doing nothing. Resist the urge to snap back at your boss in public until you have adequately assessed the situation unless the comment is truly egregious. If it is egregious, sometimes a simple "That's not okay to say" makes your perspective clear.

3. Talk to your boss in private afterwards to let them know that their statement was hurtful and not appropriate. If possible, engage them in conversation about the statement and determine what is appropriate moving forward.

4. Document incidents of insults, even if it's only in your own note log. Consider emailing notes to yourself so you have a time/date stamp, and keep emails that reflect the negative situations. This may be needed if you need to file a complaint.

5. If the statement is egregious, sexual, or otherwise highly inappropriate, consider contacting Human Resources immediately, even if anonymously, to ask them about the egregiousness of the situation.

6. Identify people who can provide perspective on working with your boss; for example, someone senior to you who works well with your boss or someone who previously worked with your boss. You can say something like, "Sometimes I'm not sure how to interpret what [Boss] is saying, but it doesn't feel good. Can you help me understand your experience with [Boss]?"

7. Consider asking a trusted friend or colleague for advice on how to address these situations.

8. Consider the nature of the work environment. Some organizations or units within them have a wide tolerance for "joking" behavior that you and others may consider hurtful. If this is the case, consider if this is the right unit/organization for you. At any time, if you are being targeted for your race/ethnicity, gender/gender expression, or religion, that is not acceptable.

9. If you see this insulting behavior, most likely other people see it too. Remember you are not alone.

10. Directly ask a colleague or two to stand up for you in these situations. If you each stand up for each other, your boss will begin to change (and you will have a better case with the organization that it is a widespread problem).

11. You may want to consider discussing the situation with a lawyer if you find it unsafe, excessive, persistent, or personalized. A lawyer represents only you and can help you understand your rights. If you need to find a lawyer, contact a local university law school for an inexpensive or low cost referral or Google "best employment lawyer" with the name of your town and call to ask for a free consultation.

12. If this is a persistent pattern that people treat you poorly, you may want to consider obtaining a coach or therapist who can help you through this challenge.

See also: Challenge 1: Understanding your values

Challenge 4: When and how to obtain a mentor

Challenge 9: Understanding hierarchy at work and when to go around it

Challenge 22: Difficulty saying no

Take Action: Create your game plan. Pull from suggestions above, what needs to happen first, second and third? Once you're clear on the direction you're taking, you can begin addressing this.

Challenge 57.
Boss lies

We expect people to tell the truth, and yet in business sometimes people are not truthful. These lies can range from harmless "white lies" to more severe lies that impact your daily work, reputation, or relationships with clients.

1. Remember you are responsible for your own integrity and you are not responsible for your boss's integrity.

2. Once you have identified that your boss lies, consider adjusting your expectations and do not expect them to tell the truth.

3. Know that other people at work, including your colleagues, your boss's colleagues, and your boss's boss probably also know about your boss's lack of honesty.

4. Find a trusted colleague with whom you can do "reality checks" after a meeting to ensure you are interpreting correctly.

5. Take good notes in meetings, and in the last few minutes of the meeting, repeat back what your boss asked you to do. If your boss later claims you interpreted incorrectly, you can refer to your notes. (Understand that this may not help.)

6. Read *The Asshole Survival Guide: How to Deal with People who Treat you Like Dirt* by Robert I. Sutton (details listed in the "For further reading" section) for how to approach your difficult person.

7. Identify someone who works with difficult people and ask them how they manage it.

8. If you see that your boss lies, most likely other people see this too, even if they can't discuss it with you. Remember you are not alone.

9. Talk to someone you trust outside of work for an external opinion.

10. If you feel your boss's lies are negatively affecting your reputation or your future, you may want to consider whether working for someone else would be better for you.

11. You may want to consider obtaining a coach who can help you through this challenge.

See also: Challenge 4: When and how to obtain a mentor

Challenge 5: When and how to obtain a career coach

Challenge 9: Understanding hierarchy at work and when to go around it

Challenge 13: How to have difficult conversations

Take Action: Is this a career you'd like to stay in? If yes, find a solution as soon as you can. If not, perhaps this might be a nudge to find another career/position? Consider sites like Indeed.com or consulting with trusted friends to see what else is available for you.

Challenge 58.
Boss has temper tantrums

Stomping feet, turning red in the face, shouting and waving arms: Not just for toddlers, unfortunately! I have witnessed grown adults have complete temper tantrums at work because something didn't go their way.

1. Stay calm. Keep your face neutral and be patient to wait for the tantrum to be over.

2. If the person throws items or in any other way makes you feel unsafe, get up and leave.

3. Be aware of people in the room who are more junior than you; make sure they are protected.

4. Consider options for interrupting the temper tantrum: a) saying calmly and slowly, "I'm happy to discuss this with you later," b) saying calmly and slowly, "Please stop yelling so we can solve the problem," or c) waiting for it to pass.

5. Your job likely does not require you to be subjected to a difficult work environment engendered by someone having frequent screaming tantrums. If it happens once or more than once, you can go to Human Resources to ask for assistance.

6. Identify someone senior to you who works well with your boss and ask them how they manage when your boss gets upset.

7. Document incidents of tantrums, even if it's only in your own note log. Consider emailing notes to yourself so you have a time/date stamp, and keep emails that reflect the negative situations. This may be needed if you need to file a complaint.

8. Identify people who previously worked with your boss and ask them for tips in how to manage your boss's moods.

9. Talk to someone you trust outside of work for an outside opinion.

10. If this continues or is egregious, you may want to consider obtaining a coach who can help you through this challenge.

11. Consider if you want to raise the stakes by saying calmly, "You are creating a hostile work environment and I need you to stop." Be aware that the phrase "hostile work environment" has a specific legal meaning that suggests you are considering escalating this to legal action. Talk with your own lawyer before making this move. If you need to find a lawyer, contact a local university law school for an inexpensive or low cost referral or Google "best employment lawyer" with the name of your town and call to ask for a free consultation.

See also: Challenge 4: When and how to obtain a mentor

Challenge 5: When and how to obtain a career coach

Challenge 9: Understanding hierarchy at work and when to go around it

Challenge 13: How to have difficult conversations

Take Action: Replay a scene in your mind of a boss's temper tantrum. What could have gone better? Knowing what you know now, how would you address the situation differently? Remember, It's not your fault and you can always seek help to remedy the situation.

Challenge 59.
Boss has a short attention span

I once worked with a boss who could not manage more than three items on an agenda or presentation slide. This boss was very smart but had a short attention span and little attention for details. A boss with a short attention span can make it challenging to work through complex problems. They also require different modes of communication for you to be effective.

1. Adjust your expectations for the kinds of conversations you can have with your boss. Keep it simple.

2. Bring an agenda to meetings with only three or four items on it and plan to focus on the most important item you need them to provide feedback or guidance on.

3. Identify someone who is effective at working with your boss and ask for suggestions for improving your approach.

4. Keep communication short: Keep all emails less than three lines and do not send your boss long missives when at all possible.

5. Offer the option of the "long version" or the "short version" of the story. They'll usually pick the short version.

6. Consider a balance between what you need your boss's input on to move forward, what is just a heads up for your boss, and what they don't need to know. Keep your conversations focused on information you and they need to know.

7. Periodically check in with your boss about how your regular conversations are going. If your boss thinks they're going well, then consider finding other ways to get what you need.

8. Consider discussing challenging issues with a trusted colleague first (or the boss's second-in-charge if available) and then simplifying to the main points for the discussion with your boss.

9. Consider whether your boss has any items that trigger their attention. Most bosses, for example, pay attention when discussing money, whether it's extra money to be saved, costs to be cut, or anticipated extra costs. Consider framing your points around these particular areas. It is good training to learn skills of how to frame and advocate for initiatives and projects.

10. Observe how other people work with your boss on complicated issues and how your boss responds. Learn from others.

11. Share details with your boss's assistant or second-in-charge, and share only the main points with your boss. That way, when your boss has questions, their assistant can often help fill in the gaps.

See also: Challenge 4: When and how to obtain a mentor
Challenge 8: Starting a new job
Challenge 13: How to have difficult conversations

Take Action: What tip stuck out the most? How can you use it the next time your boss isn't paying attention? You might become more of an asset in their eyes as you can help them keep their attention.

Challenge 60.
Don't feel supported by boss

I have been lucky enough to have significant support in various work positions. Most times, though, when I did not get that support from my official "boss," I found it from others whom I sought out or who found me. Support likely exists, if you can find it.

1. Read books on mentoring to understand what mentoring should look like and how to obtain it, especially books written by people in your field (see a few suggestions in the "For further reading" section).

2. Consider whether your expectations for feeling support at work are reasonable; it's not reasonable to expect full support all the time from your boss.

3. Ensure you have support from friends and family members outside of work. If this is a difficult time, ask them for extra help.

4. During moments where you feel particularly unsupported, write down the context and how you would like to feel instead. Once you have some examples, see if you can identify patterns in what makes you feel unsupported and in what you need. See if you can find what you need elsewhere.

5. What would it take for you to feel supported? Consider asking directly for what you need from your boss. Understand they may not be willing or able to provide it, and that they do not have to provide it.

6. If it's appropriate, ask for more frequent check-ins or feedback meetings with your boss.

7. Clarify your short- and long-term goals and identify what support you would like and who might be able to provide that support.

8. Identify other people who seem to have support from their bosses and ask them how they do it.

9. Start mentoring others. Even if you feel like you have little to give, you might be surprised at how much you have in common with others and how much better you feel when you're helping others.

10. You may want to consider obtaining a coach who can help you through this challenge.

11. Remember you are responsible for finding support. It would be nice if your boss supported you as much as you'd like, but ensure you can connect with your own supportive colleagues and friends.

See also: Challenge 13: How to have difficult conversations

Challenge 31: Want to increase influence

Challenge 38: You feel like you are not heard

Challenge 50: Boss doesn't lead

Take Action: What does your boss need? Do you see something that he/she would benefit from? Perhaps a time-saver or money generator that you could bring up in your next meeting? By you helping them, they often want to help you, too. Write out 3-5 ideas that you could offer.

Challenge 61.
Don't have resources to complete work

Sometimes you need a little more help or resources to do the work that is requested. When this happens, there are ways to get the resources you need.

1. Remember that resources can be obtained in many ways: formally through a contract or official agreement, informally talking with a colleague or friend, trading resources to another group who has what you need if you have what they need, calling in favors, and many more.

2. Clarify with your boss what the assignment requires, and ask questions about the resources available. Request the resources you need, and if the answer is no, ask how you can best identify those resources to get the job done.

3. Talk to someone who is doing similar work to find out what resources they have. You can either make a case that others have more resources to request more, or you can find novel ways to get the work done with fewer resources.

4. If the resource you need is knowledge or know-how, ask around to find out what you need to know. Your organization may pay for a portion of education that contributes to your job, have contracts with online learning systems, or offer continuing education for free.

5. Consider sharing with your boss a plan for completing the assignment and using that opportunity to ask how to manage what you perceive to be resource shortages.

6. Be careful if you always make things happen without resources; the expectation will be set that you don't need much and that you can always magically pull a rabbit out of a hat. On the other hand, if you can work efficiently, share that information with your boss and colleagues.

7. Ask around to assess what the norm is in your unit or in your organization. For example, in most fields it's expected that for professional travel, staff have hotel rooms to themselves and are not expected to share rooms with each other. Clarifying what the norm is will help you make a case to ask for what you need.

8. Sometimes extending the deadline will give you time to rustle up the resources you need. Ask if it is a possibility to have some more time.

9. Confer with a trusted colleague to see if your perceptions of resource shortages are accurate.

10. Review previous documents that might be available from your predecessor to see how they managed similar situations.

11. If you are always under-resourced, consider if this is the right position or organization for you.

See also: Challenge 4: When and how to obtain a mentor

Challenge 13: How to have difficult conversations

Challenge 21: Want to improve time management/ organization

Take Action: Jot down a list of resources that are available to you, including colleagues, funding, supplies, or something else. What can you take action on now?

Challenge 62.
Boss has unreasonable expectations

Bosses are well known for wanting things done immediately. But what do you do when the expectations don't seem to be reasonable for the assignment and for what you can realistically do?

1. Check with your boss about whether your perceptions of their expectations are accurate. Are they asking you to be responsible for the completion of the project or just to manage it? Ensure your authority to complete the project is in line with the responsibility you're being asked to take on the project.

2. Consider whether your boss is trying to challenge you and doesn't realize you are so stressed.

3. Ask a colleague to pitch in to help and offer to repay the favor. Note this can only be done a few times and is not a long-term solution.

4. Track your effort on a project through a project management workplan, share with your boss periodically, and ask your boss to help you understand where you might be able to increase your efficiency. The workplan can clarify a timeline and enable you to request additional resources sooner rather than later if tasks need additional time or resources to complete. Having a timeline also allows you to provide options; for example, "If it's just me working on this, I can have it finished in one month. If I have some assistance we can complete it in two weeks. What would you prefer?" (See resources on project management and workplans listed in the "For further reading" section.)

5. Consider sharing a plan with your boss a plan for completing your work and using that opportunity to ask how to manage

what you perceive to be expectations that may be too high.

6. Let your boss know you want to meet their high expectations, and request specific training or advice to help you do so.

7. Consider meeting with others at your level of experience and seniority and comparing job duties, expectations, etc. You can also develop this meeting into an informal mentoring group.

8. Consider whether you have changed your productivity level? Sometimes we reprioritize our lives and it impacts work. If this is the case, communicate new boundaries with your boss and see if you can negotiate how to best move forward.

9. Check with a trusted colleague regarding what expectations would be reasonable for someone with your experience and seniority. Ask your boss for help on the project, either a colleague to assist or someone more senior to help you understand all the steps so you can complete similar projects yourself next time.

10. If your boss continues to have unreasonable expectations despite your efforts to address them, consider whether this is the right job, field, or organization for you at this time.

See also: Challenge 13: How to have difficult conversations
             Challenge 20: Feel overwhelmed
             Challenge 29: Want feedback on work performance

Take Action: Communication is key, wouldn't you agree? Write out a sample email of what you wish to say to your boss about your expectations. Walk away for a bit, let it digest and return with fresh eyes. Where do you need help now? Make a plan and stick with it.

Challenge 63.
Boss undermines you

Sometimes your boss may say they support you in private and then in public they undermine you by not giving you proper credit, blaming you for problems, or suggesting indirectly that you are not good at your job.

1. Consider talking with your boss about the organization's and their perspectives on civility and courtesy generally to see if they have self-awareness and will be open to the conversation.

2. When an undermining situation happens, have a discussion with your boss about your perceptions of the situation. Ask for their opinion. They may not realize it came across that way or had that effect.

3. Identify what you observed and ask for their perspective, such as by saying, "It seemed like this was intentional; can you help me understand what happened?" Most people should respond kindly and attempt to make the situation better. If they don't, that raises a big red flag.

4. Observe the environment where you work to identify if undermining is a common and accepted occurrence or whether it is generally discouraged. If it is a common and accepted occurrence, consider whether this is the right work environment for you.

5. Consider what your boss's motive might be – is it personal to them, are they threatened by you, or is this just their way of acting? Understanding their motives may help you understand how to counter them and protect yourself.

6. Do not give them any more information about yourself, your feelings, or your inner life so they have less information to use against you.

7. Be sure you do not undermine others intentionally or unintentionally.

8. Consider meeting with colleagues to compare experiences. You can also develop this meeting into an informal mentoring group.

9. If it is possible, consider switching groups or teams in your organization so you are not working with the underminer.

10. Read *The Asshole Survival Guide: How to Deal with People who Treat you Like Dirt* by Robert Sutton (details listed in the "For further reading" section).

11. Consider whether it may make sense to limit your public expressions of disappointment or hurt. Sometimes it is better to not give people like this the satisfaction.

12. Consider whether it would be useful to bring up the scenario in a casual way. For example, if your boss asked you to lead a project then identified someone else as the lead in public, a casual way to address would be, "I was surprised you said Juan is the lead of this project in [meeting] when last week you asked me to lead it. Can you help me understand?"

13. Talk to someone you trust outside of work for an outside opinion.

14. When your boss chronically undermines you, it's really hard to overcome that and be successful at work. Consider whether it's time to move on, what you want to learn/accomplish before you leave this job, and how to start making change.

See also: Challenge 1: Understanding your values

Challenge 2: Building your network

Challenge 9: Understanding hierarchy at work and when to go around it

Challenge 36: You think it's time to move on

Take Action: Is this the right job for you? Does this fit in with your goals/dreams? Time is the most precious thing we have, do you want to mend the issue and continue or seek new employment? The choice is always yours.

Challenge 64.
Boss suggests it's time to move on

The moment may feel like a punch in the gut: Your boss suggests its time to move on. It's usually best to not fight it but rather to take it as a clear sign that you need to move on. Take your time as you can and consider your options. You likely have quite a few.

1. Remember: Careers are long. Although it may feel like the end of the world, it is not. You will go on to have wonderful adventures if you choose.

2. Ask your boss if you're being fired or being asked for a voluntary resignation. These have different implications for how you can proceed; you have more power in the situation if you are being asked for a resignation than if you are being fired for cause.

3. Let your boss know you would like some time to process the information they are sharing. Arrange to have a follow-up meeting in a few days. Go to the follow-up meeting with a plan, timeline, and questions.

4. If possible, clarify a timeline for moving on that works for you and allows you time to find another job or make plans.

5. Ask whether you are being let go for cause, for poor performance, or because of something else (budgeting, restructuring). Know your boss may not be able to tell you, but ideally can give you information that will be helpful for you as you consider next steps.

6. Update your resume to reflect your recent accomplishments. If you are having trouble thinking of any, identify goals you can

pursue and create accomplishments you will have in several months.

7. Identify if your boss's decision is final or if there are additional things you can do to increase your value to the organization.

8. Ask to speak with Human Resources to identify issues like health insurance transfer, 401k transfer, severance pay, and last paycheck.

9. Consider making a list of next steps you will need to take, such as managing your finances, finding another job, getting a roommate, or other activities that can help you in the short term. Consider both short-term methods to increase your income and reduce your outflows of money.

10. Ask your boss for a recommendation or permission to contact them for a recommendation in the future if you believe they will provide a positive one. If you are being let go for poor performance, it likely won't be helpful for you to request a recommendation from them.

11. You may want to consider obtaining a coach who can help you through a career transition.

See also: Challenge 3: Setting goals and priorities

Challenge 13: How to have difficult conversations

Challenge 36: You think it's time to move on

Take Action: Need support? Jump inside the Lead with Wisdom Community for Millennials at https://www.facebook.com/groups/295731811374991/ for support in this transition. We might even have connections for you to explore! All is not lost, look at this as a new and exciting beginning.

Challenge 65.
New boss

A new boss could be a blessing or a curse. It could mean a new start or a new challenge. You can always make the most of it.

1. Expect that there will be changes, both good and bad. This may be an opportunity to pursue projects or changes that were not possible under your previous boss. Go slowly and see how things unfold before you come to conclusions.

2. Get to know your new boss and offer to be helpful.

3. Research your incoming boss by reviewing their posts and profile on professional social media (such as LinkedIn) and asking around to understand their strengths and limitations.

4. Proactively offer your new boss a summary of your activities to date and bring a copy of the organizational chart when you start discussing people so they can more quickly learn who is who. Be prepared to let them know what is working well and where things can be improved.

5. Suggest people who might be helpful for your boss to meet with. You could also suggest people who would be very helpful for them as they adjust to their new role.

6. Limit or eliminate saying "This was how [old management] did it." No new boss likes that. You may be able to ask questions about a new change, such as, "Could you help me understand what you'd like to see different as a result of this change?" or share possible implications of a new change: e.g., "When this group considered doing that, we were concerned about

[implication]. Can we talk about how we can best address [implication]?"

7. Be available to your boss and respond quickly so that you can get started on the right foot with them. If you work from home, consider having somewhat more in-person time initially.

8. Within the first 90 days, set up a discussion with your boss about your career direction to solicit your boss's advice and make them an advocate.

9. Offer to be a resource to help the new boss or their team address the transition.

10. When you're in meetings with your new boss, be sure you've introduced them to everyone in the room, and speak up frequently so they can get to know you better.

11. Speak positively of your boss to your colleagues, and don't tolerate them badmouthing your new boss or questioning the new boss's acumen.

12. You may want to consider obtaining a coach who can help you through this challenge.

See also: Challenge 8: Starting a new job
            Challenge 10: Building relationships with colleagues
            Challenge 27: Hard to make small talk

Take Action: Pro tip, during the first week of employment see who would like to join you for coffee or lunch, It's a great way to integrate into the new environment and get to know your boss - and for your boss to get to know you.

Challenge 66.
Not sure where to go for help with a problem

If you're stumped with what you think is a completely unique problem, help is on the way! There are lots of ways to identify solutions for your unique set of circumstances.

1. Google the problem to see if anyone has addressed it online, and identify who they went to for help.

2. Find online forums related to your problem, such as Reddit or Quora.

3. Don't blame yourself if you're not sure how to address a problem; sometimes there are larger political forces at work of which you are only seeing a small part. Still try to address your part in a way that is consistent with your.

4. Identify a colleague who seems to always know where to go with problems and ask for advice.

5. Talk to someone you trust outside of work for an external opinion on the problem.

6. Identify a similar problem that may have related solutions; for example, office friendships gone bad may have some similar solutions to office romances gone bad.

7. Consider waiting if waiting won't cause irreparable damage; sometimes problems work themselves out. If you do this, make a note of how long you should wait before you revisit the issue.

8. Clarify the problem in writing, identify some possible solutions, and then try one.

9. Gather some friends for coffee or lunch and ask them to help you brainstorm solutions. This also will remind you of what's important, and how much support you have. It will help put the problems in perspective.

10. Identify books with characters who face and overcome significant problems. Although it might not give you a specific solution, it can increase your confidence that you will be able to deal with this particular problem.

11. Consider contacting a mentor, coach, or therapist about the problem.

See also: Challenge 1: Understanding your values

Challenge 3: Setting goals and priorities

Challenge 4: When and how to obtain a mentor

Challenge 5: When and how to obtain a career coach

Challenge 20: Feel overwhelmed

Take Action: If you have a problem you can't solve, write me at Jennifer@leadwithwisdom.com! I'm happy to help you figure out an answer!

For further reading

These references include some of my favorites and some recent books that can help you along on your journey toward success and respect. Share your favorites at the Lead with Wisdom Community for Millennials, https://www.facebook.com/groups/295731811374991/ or send to me at Jennifer@leadwithwisdom.com.

Productivity and Project Management

1. Getting Things Done: The Art of Stress-Free Productivity by David Allen. (New York, Penguin Books, 2015).

2. The 7 Habits of Highly Effective People: Powerful Lessons in Personal Change by Steven R. Covey. (New York, Free Press, 2004).

3. How to Shine at Work by Linda R. Dominguez. (New York, McGraw-Hill, 2003).

4. Project Management for the Unofficial Project Manager by Kory Kogon, Suzette Blakemore, and James Wood. (Dallas, TX, BenBella Books, 2015).

5. What You Need to Know about Project Management by Fergus O'Connell. (West Sussex, England, Capstone, 2011).

6. Gantt Charts for project management. www.ganttchart.com

7. Project Management Institute. www.pmi.org

Communication and Negotiation

1. Perfect Phrases for Dealing with Difficult People by Susan F. Benjamin. (New York, McGraw-Hill, 2008).

2. Emotional Vampires: Dealing with People Who Drain You Dry by Albert J. Bernstein. (New York, McGraw-Hill, 2001).

3. Influence: Science and Practice by Robert B. Cialdini. (Boston, Pearson, 2003).

4. Influence without Authority by Allan R. Cohen & David L. Bradford. (New York, John Wiley & Sons, 1991).

5. Getting to Yes: Negotiating Agreement without Giving In by Robert Fisher & William Ury. (New York, Penguin Books, 2011).

6. Bargaining with the Devil: When to Negotiate, When to Fight by Robert Mnookin. (New York, Simon & Schuster, 2010).

7. No More Team Drama: Ending the Gossip, Cliques, and Other Crap that Damage Workplace Teams by Joe Mull. (CreateSpace Independent Publishing Platform, 2018).

8. Difficult Conversations: How to Discuss What Matters Most by Douglas Stone, Bruce Patton & Sheila Heen. (New York, Penguin, 2010).

9. Stop Complainers and Energy Drainers by Linda Swindling. (Hoboken, NJ, John Wiley & Sons, 2013).

10. The Asshole Survival Guide: How to Deal with People who Treat you Like Dirt by Robert I. Sutton. (New York, Houghton Mifflin Harcourt, 2017)

Personal Growth and Change

1. What Do You Want to Do When You Grow Up? Starting the Next Chapter of Your Life by Dorothy Cantor. (Boston, Little, Brown and Company, 2001).

2. Power of Habit: Why We Do What We Do in Life and Business by. New York, Random House, 2014).

3. What Got You Here Won't Get You There by Marshall Goldsmith. (New York, Hyperion, 2007).

4. What's Stopping You? Why Smart People Don't Always Reach Their Potential and How You Can by Robert Kelsey. (West Sussex, U.K., Capstone Publishing Limited, 2011).

5. Fear and other Uninvited Guests by Harriet Lerner. (New York, HarperCollins, 2004).

6. Personal Development for Smart People: The Conscious Pursuit of Personal Growth by Steve Pavlina. (Carlsbad, CA, Hay House, 2008).

7. Tiny Beautiful Things: Advice on Love and Life from Dear Sugar by Cheryl Strayed. (New York, Vintage, 2012).

Management and Politics

1. Managing to Change the World: The Nonprofit Manager's Guide to Getting Results by Alison Green & Jerry Hauser. (San Francisco, Jossey-Bass, 2012).

2. Ask a Manager: How to Navigate Clueless Colleagues, Lunch-Stealing Bosses, and the Rest of Your Life at Work by Alison Green. (New York, Ballantine Books, 2018).

3. Managing with Power: Politics and Influence in Organizations by Jeffery Pfeffer. (Boston, Harvard Business School Press, 1992).

4. Survival of the Savvy: High Integrity Political Tactics for Career and Company Success by Rick Brandon & Marty Seldman. (New York, Free Press, 2004).

5. Good to Great: Why Some Companies Make the Leap ... and Others Don't by Jim Collins. (New York, HarperCollins Publishers, 2001).

6. Built to Last: Successful Habits of Visionary Companies by Jim Collins & Jerry I. Porras. (New York, HarperCollins Publishers, 2002).

7. The Secret Handshake: Mastering the Politics of the Business Inner Circle by Kathleen Kelley Reardon. (New York, Doubleday, 2000).

8. It's All Politics: Winning in a World where Hard Work and Talent Aren't Enough by Kathleen Kelley Reardon. New York, Doubleday, 2005).

Millennial Issues

1. The Millennial Money Fix: What You Need to Know About Budgeting, Debt, and Finding Financial Freedom by Douglas Boneparth & Heather Boneparth. (Wayne, NJ, Career Press, 2017).

2. Stuff Every Graduate Should Know: A Handbook for the Real World (Stuff You Should Know) by Alyssa Favreau. (New York, Quirk Books, 2016).

3. Broke Millennial: Stop Scraping By and Get Your Financial Life Together by Erin Lowry. (New York, TarcherPerigree, 2017).

4. "Digital Natives, Digital Immigrants." By Marc Prensky. Available at Marcprensky.com.

5. Millennial Money Makeover: Escape Debt, Save for Your Future, and Live the Rich Life Now by Conor Richardson. (Wayne, NJ, Career Press, 2019).

6. Choose Your Own Adulthood: A Small Book about the Small Choices that Make the Biggest Difference by Hal Runkel. (Austin, TX, Greenleaf Book Group Press, 2017).

7. I Will Teach You to Be Rich, Second Edition: No Guilt. No Excuses. No B.S. Just a 6-Week Program That Works by Ramit Sethi. (New York, Workman Publishing Company, 2019).

8. How to Skimm Your Life by The Skimm. (New York, Ballantine Books, 2019).

Women

1. Women Don't Ask: The High Cost of Avoiding Negotiation – and Positive Strategies for Change by Linda Babcock & Sara Laschever. (New York, Bantam Dell, 2007).

2. Ask For it: How Women Can Use the Power of Negotiation to Get What They Really Want by Linda Babcock & Sara Laschever. (New York, Bantam Dell, 2009).

3. She Wins, You Win: The Most Important Strategies for Making Women More Powerful by Gail Evans. (New York, Penguin. 2003).

4. Nice Girls Don't Get the Corner Office by Lois P. Frankel. (New York, Warner Books, 2004).

5. Be Your Own Mentor: Strategies from Top Women on the Secrets of Success by Sheila Wellington & Catalyst. (New York, Random House, 2001).

Acknowledgements

This book is the product of many years of work experience. I am grateful to my colleagues, supervisors, students, friends, and clients past and present who have shared their ideas on managing work challenges effectively and gracefully. Through our collective experiences, we have seen beautiful and inspiring examples of boss and employee integrity, persistence, and grace. We have also witnessed quite a few examples of what *not* to do. We learn from all of it how we want to approach the world and what kind of people we want to be.

Fantastic consultants provided perspective on earlier versions of this book including Valerie Weaver, Takiyah Johnson, Alison Feuer, Heather Gerould, Sacha Fernandez, Remy Watts, Jenna Van Leeuwen, Philip Moore, and Dick Kilburg.

I wish to thank Leila Creative and Webnista for cover design, Deana Riddle at Bookstarter for book design, David Aretha for editing, Martha Bullen for marketing advice, Diego G. Diaz for photography, and Seana Barbes for extensive and exquisite administrative assistance.

I appreciate my team of Katrina Amaro, Lourdes Blanco, and Tara Amato for unending support, encouragement, and puns. I am grateful to Ally, Linda, Shawn, Prea, Kristina, Michelle, Rachel, Annie and Kim, Caroline, and Priti.

I am greatly indebted to the late, incredible Martie Sucec for her editing over the past 20 years. Her advice on writing and life continues to serve me well.

I especially appreciate my mother, who taught me how to multitask and not let anything stop me, and Chuck, for consistent encouragement and cheering.